Christy —

All good wishes

Gunter Help

Oct. 2012

1

# NOT LOST FOR WORDS

## Gunter Helft

## CONTENTS

# DEDICATIONS

Dear Steph and Jo, Grace and Freddie, in England, and, in Australia, Sophie, Harry, Lucy, Millie and Phoebe. This book is dedicated to you.

There is a great age gap between you, so you will all read your copy at different times, most of you long after I am no longer around. In earlier times you'd have grown up surrounded by relations- grandparents, uncles, aunts, cousins- and you'd have heard stories about your family, anecdotes told about relatives long dead or grandparents' childhood memories. You would have a much stronger sense of where you belong in the history of the tribe. Nowadays, families are spread out across the world as ours is, and even those living in the same country don't see each other all that much. But I know that most of us, as we get a bit older, want to know more - who were my grandparents? Where did they live? What became of their other children? Where do I fit into the larger picture?

Not all family histories are as interesting as ours, involving different countries, different religions, persecutions, death camps, migrations. Your background is unusual, you ought to be aware of it and, hopefully, you will find it enriching.

I hope you will plough your way through these chapters and find something of interest. But I have to confess that not all of it is written just for you. There are others who have expressed an interest in my life story and some of this book is addressed to them as much as to you. I have been told it will also be of interest to some whom I do not know personally but who share experiences with me - adoption, cancer, or becoming Christian from some other background. I have in mind too all those who have encouraged me to write.

There has been a television series *Who Do You Think You Are* in which people conducted research into their ancestors, building a picture of their background. Here's your version – Enjoy!

# SOME EXPLANATORY NOTES

My younger readers may not know that the Soviet Union (Russia and its satellite countries) played a significant role in winning the Second World War. On Germany's eastern front Russians showed great courage and sacrifice, for example in the siege of Stalingrad. Their army was then the first to enter Berlin in 1945 and for the next 44 years Europe was carved up between the communist bloc of the East – Russia, Poland, Hungary, Bulgaria, Romania, etc. and the West – Britain, France, Holland, Belgium, the Scandinavian countries etc. with the USA as rich Big Brother exercising a not always welcome influence. Berlin was divided by a great wall and Germany became two separate states. There was great hostility between the two blocs, with threats and counter threats. Winston Churchill coined the phrase 'iron curtain' to describe this situation which dominated world affairs until the collapse of the Soviet Union and the reunification of Germany in 1989.

In several parts of the book the word *assimilation* appears frequently. It simply means to be fully absorbed by the life style or customs or beliefs of a group, country or nation to which one had not previously belonged – e.g. Jews in pre-Nazi Germany becoming fully German rather than Jewish in their lifestyle, or a Jew becoming a Christian, a German becoming British. **Diaspora** means scattering and refers to the history of the Jewish people ever since their eviction from Judaea.

In those parts of the book in which I refer to matters relating to Christianity, the words *anglican* and *anglicanism* mean Church of England and sometimes those churches which together with the Church of

England form a world-wide communion of churches – as in my reference to the *Nippon Seiko Kai* (the anglican church in Japan).

Christianity has Protestant and Catholic Churches. The anglican communion has for historical and theological reasons an affiliation to both. In writing of the Church of England I have used the word ***evangelical*** to refer to those at the Protestant or 'low church' end of the church; others, like me, are 'high church' and 'anglo catholic'. If none of this means anything to you, don't let it bother you! This is the kind of book in which some sections will interest some readers while other bits will leave them totally cold. You can't please all the people all the time!

**Acknowledgement: My thanks to Emma Henderson whose cheerful enthusiasm and bright ideas have helped me to focus on the latter stages of preparing the book for publication and without whose hard work and skill in the practical things it would not have been completed.**

# INTRODUCTION

Only the famous and the infamous can reasonably expect that others would want to read the story of their lives. Perhaps they have done interesting things that have been in the public domain and interacted with well-known people. Their life stories help us to see what has made them into the kind of men and women whom we see on film or stage, or about whom we have read in the newspapers. Their books give us an insight into the events of our time. Not least, their autobiographies nourish our innate curiosity, feeding our hunger for gossip and scandal. As for their motives in writing, such books are, of course, by definition egocentric; they are often self-serving, sometimes not strictly truthful or, at best, show selective memory. We, the readers, accept this is so and read on.

I am neither famous, nor, I hope, infamous. What arrogance, what extremes of egotism, it may well be asked, would lead me to write about my life let alone think others would want to read about it? Well, blame my friends. For many years I have repeatedly been told that my life has been so unusual, some of my experiences so out of the ordinary, that I should give an account of it and that it would be of interest to some who have never heard of me. Now, when I shall be ninety at my next birthday, after sixty-three years of ordained ministry and of surviving twenty-nine years after being told I only had about three months to live, I have finally knuckled down to this task and offer these recollections and reflections.

Inevitably there is some chronological order in this book. That is necessary to give it a certain logical shape. However, it is by and large totally unimportant to record what I did on the third Thursday of November in a given year. I have tried, rather, to present themes which together make up the strands of my life. Perhaps these themes and fragments may echo the experiences of others, although not everyone will agree with the reflections and comments I offer.

There have been two major events in my life that together have contributed to the title of this book. I was totally 'lost for words', but not for long, when I came to this country as a ten year old 'refugee'. Some of the book addresses the concept of assimilation, of learning new languages in different situations; by the Jews in pre-Nazi Germany, by those adopted as children and their adoptive parents, by immigrants, by those who change their religion, by natural rebels who hold 'establishment' positions. Language has since earliest childhood been of great importance to me. This is reflected in my attitude to all these different things that have formed part of my life.

The other real 'loss of words' deals with the experience of throat cancer, the strange reality of terminal illness, the complete loss of voice, the acquiring and use of oesophageal speech, having a language but not having the tools to use it.

I have also tried to reflect on the languages that I have heard and developed in education, in politics and in my theological beliefs. It did not, therefore, seem extraneous to include a chapter on the Sixties, that most exciting of decades, and to address that which I find depressing in the post-socialist world in which we now live.

Much of my working life has been devoted to developing and trying to put into practice a philosophy of education. My book *From the Head Upwards,* which was published in 2001, is devoted to what I believe about the leadership, management and structure of schools. This area is therefore only briefly addressed in the present book.

In a way I have fulfilled part of my earlier definition of autobiographies. It is self-serving in that I have enjoyed writing it. I can only hope that readers will enjoy it too. When I left my headship in Doncaster a colleague generously said, 'his epitaph will always be that he made us think'. I hope that this is true, and that this book will provoke some thought.

**Who else?**

When the self-important confront the aggressive, they are challenged with 'You and who else?' What army of witnesses, they are asked, is going to make us take you seriously? I must now put this book into the context of my 'army', which some may consider a strange analogy for me to use as a pacifist!

Dr Peter Selby, at his installation as Bishop of Worcester, spoke of the 'but-for-whoms', those without whose influence and support we would not have done what we have or be where we are. Because this book is more thematic than simply chronological, I have not given a fair account of those by whose very existence my life is defined.

By the nature of the themes I have chosen, my parents and their role are fairly fully described. Similarly, I have been able to show the influence of some who have been my teachers and mentors. A few of those who have been my colleagues over the years are mentioned more or less in passing. Some of them have exercised a much greater influence on my life than might be apparent in these pages; I must not introduce this book without acknowledging my deep indebtedness to them. Although they may not wish to be mentioned by name, I hope they know who they are.

The great omission from much of what I have written is my wife Diane. I do describe how we met and the circumstances of our marriage. This book would not have been written if she had not been there in the last fifty-nine years. She is my great 'but-for-whom'. I cannot conceive how I could have been without her in Japan, or in the jobs in Oxford and London, or in school headships. In fact, and other happily married people will echo this from their own lives, I just cannot imagine how there could have been a life without her. In everything to which I may refer in these pages Diane has played a much greater part than onlookers may sometimes have recognised. Life would be terribly boring if we had always agreed, never agued, or even never hurt each other. We are, however, among those lucky few whose marriage has withstood all that and matured through it. There has been better and worse, richer and poorer, sickness and health over our years together. I am very blessed that our love has endured it all for so long. Those who know us will recognise that the 'bravery awards' in all this are Diane's, not mine.

There is in this book virtually no mention of our sons, Michael and Peter. Those who saw me only in the role of priest or of head teacher, might not necessarily have seen me in that of husband, and so too my being a parent may have seemed extraneous to my work. But, of course, it was not. We do not go to work without bringing the whole of ourselves to whatever has to be done that day. Michael's severe childhood asthma, his youthful generosity of affection, his adult tendency to detachment, his gift to get on quietly with what has to be done and to do it effectively; Peter's vivacity and talent, his difficult adolescence, his courage and optimism in adult life - at different times all these thing have of course impinged on us as parents . Both sons have had highs and lows in their lives which we have shared to the extent they wanted them shared, but these are their stories and not for me to write about here. They are, as I write this, both in their fifties and have, at times, taught us how true it is that one doesn't worry any less about one's children even when they are older.

We were not, I think, particularly good parents. We made some fundamental errors, but this is a fairly common self-assessment of parenting it would seem. Certainly I was too much of a workaholic and our willingness to move to the right job did not always give the boys the continuity and security to which they were entitled. At least we didn't send them away to boarding school or to private day schools; and we seem to have shared with them certain basic principles to which they still adhere, though neither of them now claims to have a faith or to attend church. Sometimes, of course, they did not appreciate our ideals. They felt deprived, for example, that I would not let them play with toy guns. But now, naturally, do not like to see their own children play with such toys. When they were little we had some very happy family times. Being our children, they can both be utterly infuriating but we enjoy them and their families, missing Peter terribly, 12000 miles away in Australia. They are very different from each other. But they are also quite scarily alike which may be the reason why they have not always found it easy to get on together.

11

'Me and who else?' There have been very many but-for-whoms, but none as important as Diane, Michael and Peter.

As for grandchildren, and now great-grandchildren, they bring yet another role and dimension to one's life. To watch them grow is fascinating and a great joy. It is such a shame that we hardly know our five Australian grandchildren and never will. This book is dedicated to all the younger members of the family.

# I
## WHO AM I?

President Kennedy once famously claimed to be a Berliner. In his case, although he didn't realise   that could only mean that he was a certain type of doughnut. I, on the other hand, am a Berliner in that I was born in that city and spent the first ten years of my life there. Like most Berliners we lived in a four-story house consisting of flats. The English norm of one-family houses was virtually unknown on the continent then. For a vivid account of how these blocks of flats tended to be very socially mixed, and the dynamics of life among the tenants, I recommend a very moving novel, *Alone in Berlin* by Hans Fallada, published in English by Penguin.

I lived at Wilmersdorferstrasse 63 in the district of Charlottenburg. The house stood, by 1920's standards, on a busy intersection with Kantstrasse; there were shops at street level and department stores in the vicinity. Half a mile up the road was the famous Kurfürstendamm, Berlin's fashionable thoroughfare of shops and the centre of the café life for which Berlin's middle class and Bohemian populations were renowned. To be taken as a small boy by my parents on a Sunday afternoon to sit in a café, eat cakes and watch the world go by, listen in as they met up with friends and bumped into acquaintances, was never boring. On occasion, if I appeared to be getting restless, they'd send me off to count the number of tables or how many different coloured chairs I could see. I felt I was truly involved in the pulsing heartbeat of a vibrant and exciting city. So, to return to this chapter's title…Who Am I?

My parents were Arthur and Käte Helft. They were, in every significant sense, my parents. Yet, they were not my parents. My mother, Käte Gottfurcht, née Kristeller, died in childbirth and my father, Hans Gottfurcht, asked his sister Käte and her husband to look after my infant-self before eventually agreeing to my being adopted by them. As a very small child I called my parents' brothers, sisters and in-laws 'aunt' or 'uncle'. Only one of them was termed differently. He was called 'Papa Hans'.

When I was about four, I was told I had chosen that name for him as a baby and was now too old to use it, that I was now to call him 'uncle Hans'. I fervently wish they had not done that. Presented to them at this point, was a marvellous opportunity to tell me the truth. They could have told me that I was exceptionally lucky to have more people to love me than most children. That I belonged to them, but that Hans and his new wife Herta, née Bendinger, who had been his secretary, would always have a special role in my life, and I in theirs. They could have explained that my much loved and loving grandparents were the same, being the parents of both Käte and Hans, my adoptive mother and natural father.

Yet they did not do so. I believe that all of them were frightened and I can understand that the Helfts did not want to risk having to share me; the Gottfurchts were too insecure in their new found happiness to want the complication of an overt 'special relationship' with me. Even worse, neither couple went on to have children of their own. The Helfts were frightened of finding a difference between their attitude to a natural child and an adopted one. Hans and his wife, Herta, always incidentally my favourite 'aunt', had no children for similar reasons, and because Hans could not face Herta's exposure to all the dangers of childbirth which had robbed him of his first wife. The one couple loved me too possessively and the other with too much frustration, while I myself had throughout my childhood and adolescence a sense of deep insecurity which no one was willing to explain to me.

It was not until late in the war, when I was twenty one and in need of my birth certificate, that things came to a head. My parents tried to stall me when I asked them to send it to me, saying that they would deal with the matter for me. In fact, they couldn't; I had to be shown the certificate, everything blew wide open. It even revealed that I was registered as 'Gunter Helft-Gottfurcht. I was double barrelled!

Although I understand why I was not told as a small child, I believe that everyone concerned was dreadfully misguided. I can also understand that each year it became more difficult, the longer it was put off it let them live in a sort of denial and probably hoped I need never find out. I have not felt angry about it, because the underlying reason had much to do with a misguided desire to protect me. There were certainly some less worthy motives, but all of them very human ones, and it would be too easy to be judgemental in retrospect.

For all that, I was deeply traumatised by the revelation and I believe I was damaged by the concealment. I have found it very difficult throughout my adult life to take people's relationships with me at face value. I have had very few close friendships and I believe this is because I am afraid of letting people get too near, in case they turn out not to be what they seem. Even if none of this is directly attributable to my adoption and the way it was handled, it has made me prone to an excessive degree of introspection.

15

Two other aspects of the whole affair were, and to some extent remain, hurtful. Firstly, I found it quite astonishing that, within days of my being at last told the truth, my parents expected me to feel as though nothing had changed, while Hans expected I should think that everything had. My parents showed little comprehension of the impact of this news, while Hans wanted suddenly a new father-son relationship. No one appeared to have the slightest understanding that they had clobbered me with a terrible crisis of identity and that, melodramatic as it may sound, they had shaken the foundations on which my life had been built.

Secondly, it was hurtful to realise that my own generation in the family, my cousins on the Helft side, had known all along and been sworn to secrecy. This now made sense of the frequent snide innuendoes from one of them, which I had not understood as a child. In a fairly close knit family I had always felt like the odd man out - now I was beginning to understand why.

Finally, I have a sense of deprivation that I know so little about my real mother. Mention of her appeared to pose a threat to everyone in the family. It almost seemed that they wanted me to believe she had never existed. Later, I discovered that throughout my childhood a cold war was waged with my real mother's family, especially her sister, who perhaps understandably felt that I had been snatched from their influence. It has all left me with too many unanswered questions in the search for my identity.

As an adult I have been perceived as self-assured to the point of arrogance. I do not deny or try to excuse that. It may just be, however, that like the arrogance of so many people, mine is, at least in part, due to that deep insecurity which others do not perceive and which has its roots in this aspect of my life.

## Nature and Nurture

Arthur and Käte were an odd couple. Käte had been at school with Arthur's sisters and had become a family friend. After the First World War he set up his own business, manufacturing calendars and greetings cards, the trade to which he had been apprenticed. Käte became his secretary and office manager. They were married a few months later in 1919.

It is hard to determine what they had in common, and I gather this puzzled many of their own contemporaries. Arthur came from a self-consciously Jewish household who were first generation Berliners. They had been a prominent family in the small town of Prenzlau, North East of the German capital. Arthur's father had been banished to Holland for some never-to-be-revealed deed that had darkened the name of the dynasty, and he died there. Grandmother Helft, frail as she seemed to be, was very much the matriarch of the family. She had three sons and three daughters, all middle of the road and very middle class. I do not know how my cousins found her, for me she was someone totally remote.

My Gottfurcht grandparents require a special mention here, for the part they played in my life and the influence they had upon it. They were, after all, the parents of both my birth father and my adoptive mother and, as things turned out, I was their only grandchild. My grandmother, Auguste (née Abraham) was a gentle and, as I have already said, rather frail looking

17

woman somewhat overshadowed by her husband. I remember her only as somebody who showed me great affection. She mercifully died in February 1933, spared the dispersal of her family later that year and the dreadful things that would have befallen her, had she lived.

My grandfather, Siegmund Gottfurcht, a wine and spirits salesman (rep) was, and has remained, after my parents and my wife, the most important person in my life. I loved him dearly. That love has had a great influence over me, although some might say that I have inherited some of his less attractive characteristics. He was autocratic, pedantic, self-opinionated and, apparently, a bit of a womaniser. I remember, when I was about seven, I was allowed to walk on my own the short distance from my home to theirs. On occasion he was liable to phone my mother to say 'You said the boy would be here at three, he has only just arrived and it is seven minutes past three'. Sunday afternoon outings with him and my grandmother for coffee and cakes in a fashionable Berlin cafe with a live orchestra are among my happiest childhood memories. When we left for England in July 1933 he waved us goodbye on the station platform and I had my first experience of heartbreaking grief.

He was able to visit us in London in 1935. My parents and I begged him to stay but he said he could not live in a place where you 'could not ask a policeman for the time because he does not speak German'! So he went back to Berlin but my abiding memory is always of him standing alone on that Berlin station platform. The place was full of jackbooted thugs in Nazi uniform, yet even then we could not have foreseen how awful the persecution was to become and that nine years later, by which time he had remarried, he would, aged 78, be dragged from his bed, thrown on a train

18

and murdered in Terezin Camp in Czechoslovakia. [Like all who had relatives that perished in the Holocaust we are indebted for this detailed information to *Yad Vashem*, the amazing organisation which researches and records the full history of the *Shoa* in this great detail.]

My mother, who rebelled against her father but who was very like him, had been a very early feminist and an activist in all kinds of progressive causes. Her younger brother, Fritz, was quite a successful writer. He was very much what was termed in those days a Bohemian. His life seemed to me as a child enormously exciting and glamorous. Later, in England, he became a much respected film scriptwriter and editor, heading up the script department of ABC in their Elstree studios. This was no mean achievement, especially for someone using his writing skills in a second language, now using the name Frederick Gotfurt. In his younger days he was certainly a communist and probably an anarchist, the fashionable thing to be in post First World War Berlin. He held very left wing views until the end of his life, and he and I had a great affinity from my earliest childhood until his death.

My mother's other brother, Hans, my natural father, was a trade union official. In Berlin in the twenties he was an exceptionally young general secretary of the clerical workers' union. I remember that it greatly impressed me that he made radio broadcasts whilst we all sat around weird receivers, passing the headphones from one to the other. He attracted the attention of the Nazis very early on. For a while in 1933 he stayed every night at a different address in order to evade arrest. Eventually he spent a short time in Dachau concentration camp; I have never quite understood how and why he was released.

19

Hans and Herta came to London in 1936 and during the war he did some secret work to assist underground activities in Germany, preparing for the re-establishment of a free German trade union movement after the war. He became the deputy general secretary of ICFTU (the International Confederation of Free Trade Unions) in Brussels and later retired to Lugano in Switzerland. He would have been at ease with New Labour; while he always claimed to be a socialist, I found him a depressingly right wing one.

My background therefore contained a wide political spectrum. My childhood in Berlin was in a comfortable middle class home, with maids and expensive habits and attitudes; my father always advised me not to have a holiday unless I could afford at least a four star hotel! Yet, in that same home, I was sent to a Marxist elementary school, and was encouraged by my mother to join the children's section of the Social Democrats, making friends with contemporaries from quite a different social background. I was exposed to the atheist humanism of my school and of the Gottfurcht family, and, simultaneously, mixed socially with the Helft cousins and observed, albeit from a distance, the Jewish traditionalism of that grandmother.

I would be a much more interesting case study in the nature v. nurture debate, if the two strands had not been so inextricably interwoven in my daily experience. Who can say whether I am more of a Gottfurcht than a Helft because of my birth, or because, of the two Helfts, my mother, nee Gottfurcht, was the stronger personality? Or who can say that I like four star hotels because of my Helft upbringing or because I inherited the champagne socialism of my Gottfurcht grandfather and my uncle Fritz? For that matter, what do we know about the force of either nature or nurture as against the individual's development through peer groups and other external influences? We all try to establish for ourselves how much we owe to our home and how much we would have acquired on the way, regardless of family. For those who have been adopted this sort of thing becomes a bit more complex.

Over the years I have spoken with many parents of adopted children. Two things appear to emerge. Firstly, it seems clear that the earlier the fact of adoption has been openly shared with the child, the easier it has been to assure normality, mutual acceptance, and a feeling of security by both child and parents. It is only in cases like mine, where the revelation, as if of some dark and dreadful secret, has been left far too late, that all kinds of insecurities and suspicions develop. Great harm is done to the trust on which families should be based.

Secondly, there seems to me to be a pattern of complacency on the part of the adoptive parent, which cannot be quite so easily shared by the adopted child. For the parents, the trauma occurs at the time of adoption, when all sorts of doubts have to be overcome, fears assuaged. After that, they seem simply to assume that the child is theirs, finding it hard to understand why the child does not find it quite so straight forward as he or she grows up.

I have had a happy and fulfilled life, although undoubtedly it would have been less complex if my adoption had been handled in the way most, thank goodness, nowadays tend to be. Those with no personal experience in this area should never under-estimate the enormity of adopting a child, nor the difficulties it poses for most adoptees. Of course the overriding need, as in any other family, is that the child should be loved; and certainly no one could have been loved more than I was. The danger is that insecurity will lead to over-compensation and to a love that is over-possessive. There is no such thing in human relations as totally unselfish loving. In the adoption situation everyone concerned should, I believe, always question whose need they are primarily meeting in the love they bestow, and the answer to that is frighteningly complicated.

**Good Parenting**

Oscar Wilde said that children begin by loving their parents, later they understand them, and sometimes they forgive them. This chapter is full of attempts at understanding, but may appear weak on forgiving.

The prerequisite of good parenting is love and I was much loved. While mistakes were made there is a great deal for which I have to be thankful, much less to forgive. It was only through a sacrificial love that, in good times and in bad, my needs were unfailingly considered before theirs by my parents. This applied to education, holidays, clothing and all the other material concerns of family life. Emigration, of which more later, brings its fair share of difficult times.

The good parenting, to which I owe so much, went well beyond the material essentials however. My parents, for example, put much energy and devotion into introducing me to theatre, music and the arts. They shared their lives with me, excluding me from very little. From a very early age I was admitted to adult company and learned about politics, finance and the world in general from the conversations I heard. I sometimes claim that I could compete with London taxi drivers in 'the knowledge' of the streets and back alleys of the capital. Any truth in such a claim rests upon my father's eagerness to show me all the nooks and crannies of the city almost every Saturday morning in my early teens. He loved London and I have inherited that love. Both my parents took enormous trouble to share their enthusiasms with me.

Both wanted so much good for me. My mother especially was a very remarkable woman and the influence of both of them has fashioned my approach to much in life. I deeply regret that I did not show them my love as I ought to have done or let them see my sense of indebtedness to them.

My understanding of who I am would perhaps have been more complete if my natural mother had not been airbrushed so ruthlessly. Until my cousin was able to produce one recently, I had never seen a photograph of her and nobody has ever told me anything of her characteristics or temperament. What did she like and dislike? What influence did she bring to the marriage from her own family background? I am sad that I have gone through life with a total ignorance of part of who I am.

### TEREZÍNSKÁ PAMĚTNÍ KNIHA

Attach Image or Documentation

Siegmund Gottfurcht was born in 1864. During the war he was deported with Transport I/46, Train Da 502 from Berlin,Berlin,Berlin,Germany to Theresienstadt,Ghetto,Czechoslovakia on 17/08/1942. Siegmund was murdered in 1942 in Terezin, Camp. This information is based on a List of Theresienstadt camp inmates found in Terezinska Pametni Kniha/Theresienstaedter Gedenkbuch, Terezinska Iniciativa, vol. I-II Melantrich, Praha 1995, vol III Academia Verlag, Prag 2000.

| | |
|---|---|
| Source: | Terezinska Pametni Kniha/Theresienstaedter Gedenkbuch, Terezinska Iniciativa, vol. I-II Melantrich, Praha 1995, vol. III Academia Verlag, Prag 2000 |
| Last Name: | Gottfurcht |
| First Name: | Siegmund |
| Gender (according to given name): | Male |
| Date of Birth: | 10/04/1864 |
| Place of Death: | Terezin, Camp |
| Date of Death: | 31/08/1942 |
| Details of transport: | Transport I/46 , Train Da 502 from Berlin, Berlin, Berlin, Germany to Theresienstadt, Ghetto, Czechoslovakia on 17/08/1942 |
| Prisoner Nr. in Transport: | 4806 |
| Type of material: | List of Theresienstadt camp inmates |
| Victims' status end WWII: | murdered/perished |
| Item ID: | 4892863 |

# II

## "ICH BIN EIN BERLINER"

I have not lived in the place for almost 80 years. My formative years after the age of ten, all my secondary and higher education, took place in England. I became British. I served Britain in the war. I married an English girl and we brought up our two sons as British - indeed, what else could they be? I have spent an entire lifetime working in or from Britain. I get rather offended when it is suggested that I am remotely anything other than what I feel myself to be, what my passport describes as a 'British citizen'.

There is even something about the covert about me, ways in which I am more British than the British. I have the most fervent admiration for aspects of Britishness that the real native perhaps doesn't even know exist. Have I not, after all, been the recipient of this country's inherent decency, its tolerance of the stranger, its acceptance of slight eccentricity and differentness? Do I not know, because of what I have experienced, that some of today's ugly displays of bigotry, racialism and petty nationalism are aberrations, which must be corrected so that Britain may revert back to its true nature?

As for the English language, my second language, which Shaw called 'the language of Milton, Shakespeare and the Bible'; I am more of a purist than most of those who were born here. I deplore the split infinitive, which has suddenly become respectable, the use of 'who' where it should be 'whom', the awful nasal twang and careless enunciation of 'estuary English'. I cringe at the incessant repetition of meaningless words and phrases that demean the language, like 'basically' and 'at the end of the day'.

At a much more fundamental level ('basically'!) my professional interests are, of course, totally Britain-focussed. One cannot spend the whole of one's adult life involved in the country's education system, its established church, or its political activity, and feel oneself the citizen of some foreign land.

So I am, somewhat emphatically, not a Berliner. Yet, people who were born in Little Muddlecombe have a consciousness of that fact, a residual affection for it, long after they have gone to live and work in London or Glasgow. When you substitute for the name of some remote village that of a large and vibrant capital city, which was a world magnet in the years of my childhood there; when you were bought up in a family and social group which was part of that vibrancy, that special 1920's culture, and believed in sharing it with its children; then something sticks and there is a sense of being forever a Berliner.

I am British and, so long as we have nation states, I would not wish to be anything else. Yet there is in my Britishness an ingredient which must always be peculiar to my origin. My contemporaries who spent their childhood in, say, London are as metropolitan and probably as cosmopolitan as I am. But their experience is different. They did not sit with their parents in pavement cafés or witness the elegant fashions and 'Bohemian' behaviour of pre-Nazi Berlin.

At the personal level I am a Berliner because there I learnt to walk and to talk; there I had my earliest experiences of family life, of loving and being loved by parents, grandparents, uncles, aunts and cousins. There I first encountered the concept of friends and neighbours and my first day of school. Not least, there I first developed my love of language, of the use of words.

Above all, it was in Berlin that I was first exposed to some of the more awful things that can happen in life - the sudden end of joyfulness and of an element of superficiality, to be replaced by a real danger and then the traumatic upheaval of farewells and flight. I was, of course, infinitely more fortunate than so many others of my generation and background. Yet the advent of Hitler and what followed was a terrible shock to a child of 10 and, silly as it may seem to say so after nearly eighty years, it has left scars.

## A Berlin Birthday

It was April 25$^{th}$ 1933 and the eve of my 10$^{th}$ birthday, on which I had been promised a trip to the circus. I also had some fairly definite hopes in terms of presents; it was all quite exciting, so I probably wouldn't in any case have got to sleep very quickly that night.

We lived, as I have said, in a flat, albeit a pretty substantial flat, on the junction of two of the busiest thoroughfares of the inner city district of Charlottenburg. There had been great excitement a year or so earlier, when new-fangled traffic lights were installed on that corner in the form of a dial on which a large hand moved slowly from the green to the red half. From my window I could observe the stores of the Wilmersdorfer Strasse, including the first German branch of C.&A., then known by its Dutch name of C.&A. Brenningmeier. One of my earliest memories is of a crowd of frantic men and women outside the shuttered doors of the bank across the road on the day of the 1929 financial crash.

Also opposite our block was the busy pub ('Kneipe') in Kant Strasse, which was a well known haunt of Communist activists and, by 1933, a frequent and quite bloody battleground between them and marauding Nazi storm troopers. Wounding and death were fairly regular occurrences in that pub and I was quite used to be woken up by police cars and ambulances in the early hours.

From my vantage point I was also able to watch the political torch light processions, which were fashionable long before Hitler made them notorious. On my birthday there was always a special procession, with bands and flags. When I was very small I assumed it was all in my honour. In fact, I cannot remember whether they were a celebration of President Hindenburg's birthday, observed annually during his presidency, or some other notable commemoration associated with the Weimar Republic.

The walls between flats in those old Berlin buildings were very substantial. However, loud noise did carry and the night before my birthday was to be a night of never-to-be-forgotten noise.

Our neighbours in the next flat were a very charming and articulate artist, Herr Illiard, an ardent and active Communist, and his daughter Rosie, some three years younger than me. A curtain half way along the corridor divided their flat, his estranged wife occupying the other part. I do not think I ever met her, since her end of the flat opened onto the back staircase which I was not allowed to use much. She was said to have been an early member of the Nazi party, which may well have something to do with her estrangement from her husband! At about 1.30.a.m. of the night before my birthday, I became conscious of loud banging and shouting, followed by the sound of Illiard's flat door being splintered before crashing to the floor.

My parents had by now come to my room. For the following two hours, which seemed to go on forever, we heard the terrible scream of Herr Illiard as he was being systematically beaten to death, and the quite indescribable howls of little Rosie, who had been tied to a chair to witness this 'interrogation' of her father by brown shirted, jack booted Nazi thugs.

In those very early days of the Hitler regime there was still a notional difference between these storm troopers (the S.A.) and the civilian police who, it was claimed, could legitimise or prohibit such 'house searches', as these attacks were euphemistically called. Of course the police never did prohibit; even well disposed policemen did not court martyrdom. However, my father phoned the police station to ask whether this particular 'search' was legal and they promised to investigate. A police car arrived later; we heard a shot and the noises of terror resumed. Early the next morning, from the kitchen window, we saw two bodies being carried from the building by the back staircase. One was that of our neighbour. One must draw one's own conclusions about the second corpse, but it was known that, after that night, the police in the Charlottenburg district never again intervened in an S.A. operation.

I do not think that I realised at the time how courageous it had been of my parents to phone the police. As for Rosie, we saw her the next day, whimpering pitifully as she was being led away by a large woman in Nazi uniform. We were told she had been put in a children's home but were not able to find out any details, although my parents did try, again at considerable personal risk. We also tried to find Rosie again many years later when the war was over, but without success. Knowing how much I, at a relatively safe distance, was affected by the events of that night, I dread to think what it did to Rosie. Could she ever have recovered from such unspeakable trauma?

In later years I encountered a number of quite dangerous situations, but I have never again been as frightened or as deeply disturbed as I was that night in 1933. It was not as if I were, even at that age, politically innocent. I had been brought up to be conscious of the world around me and had been sent to a Marxist school. I was a member of the youngest section of the Young Socialist movement and comprehended the nuances of political left and right. I had understood for some years that, in this context, 'right' equals wrong. Yet that night has left me with recurring nightmares that still occasionally plague me all these years later, convincing me for the rest of my life of the evil of violence in pursuit of political or national interests.

The visit to the circus took place and I got my presents. Everyone made a great fuss of me, but our minds were not really focussed on birthdays and our smiles belied the trauma of the night before. Incidentally, the circus we went to see was the Circus Busch, which has only relatively recently closed, and which I was next to encounter twenty years later in, of all places, Hong Kong.

**Good Germans?**

That night was probably a watershed for my parents. We had always been on very friendly terms with the other residents in the house, some of whom owned the quite prestigious shops on the street level of our block. From then onwards however, we had to live with the knowledge that most of them had looked the other way. Nearly all of them totally refused to acknowledge what had happened and we, as a family, were ostracised as potentially dangerous neighbours who might provoke the new regime and its bully boys.

Over the years there has been endless debate about the guilt of ordinary Germans and generalisation of either kind is clearly flawed. Yet there cannot be any doubt that far too many gave in much earlier than was necessary. To say, 'they had no choice' is simply rubbish; that many lacked the guts is nearer the mark. A lot of them were decent people who did not like what they saw; but they failed to act while there was still time.

Equally, it is nonsense to pretend that 'they did not know', as so many Germans claimed after the war, wishing others to believe that they would have had no part in it if they had been aware of what was happening. If one has, for example, visited the deeply moving site of Belsen concentration camp, it is clear that the villagers of adjacent Bergen-Belsen saw, heard and smelled the atrocities on their doorstep. Not only did they know, their extended families throughout Germany knew. Our neighbours knew what was happening that night and got scared. I do not judge them; I was scared too. Yet they were responsible adults who, for the most part, were instinctively appalled by what was happening in their country. They nearly all belonged to a social group that had no need to seek solutions in violent and undemocratic ideals and their voice would have been heard if they had chosen to speak. Even in the secrecy of the ballot booth they voted for a quiet life and Hitler had gained victory in a general election in Germany in 1933.

The economic alibi is, however, more credible. There was massive unemployment and much deprivation. People had become frustrated with successive, both left of centre and centre right, Governments, which were increasingly ineffective after the defeat of the Social Democrats. The left was enfeebled by the senseless strife between the S.D.P. (Social Democratic Party) and the communists. This ideological warfare has weakened the cause of socialist politics throughout Europe ever since. Undoubtedly large sections of the German population were demoralised and disaffected, ready to look with hope on any radical alternative.

Immigration, as we know it today, was virtually unheard of; so it could not be claimed that the immigrants were 'taking our jobs, our women, and our houses'. Instead, the Jews traditionally filled the role of whipping boy. They had made a considerable contribution to the commercial and cultural life of Germany and had reaped the rewards for their efforts at a time when many Germans had not had the chance to do anything for which to be rewarded. Hitler did not need to be a genius to understand the value of anti-Semitism as an ingredient in attracting people to his programme.

We do well to reflect that violent expressions of nationalism and xenophobia are quite normal reactions to economic crisis everywhere. It is argued that there is something in the 'German character' that enabled these things to be taken to such excess. It is more likely that the claim 'it couldn't happen here' has already been partly disproved and does a great disservice to the cause of assuring that it doesn't in fact happen here.

It used to be said in the war that 'the only good German is a dead German' and clearly that is an unacceptable attitude. However, it is true that the best Germans were those who died, or risked death, in the fight again Nazism.

Had there been more of them, the world, and not least the German people themselves, would have been spared much suffering.

**In some ways I am still a Berliner**

My father had been apprenticed to his trade with the greeting card and calendar manufacturers Raphael Tuck in London before the First World War and had then done business with England throughout the 1920s and early 30s. So my parents had contemplated leaving Germany when Hitler came to power. If, by April 1933, they still had doubts about moving from their homeland, family and friends, I think the horror of the night from the 25th to 26th April did much to make up their minds.

For many years after the war, and when the world discovered the full enormity of what had happened in Germany under Hitler, I felt revulsion at the mere thought of ever going there again. My parents went on a short visit in about 1947 to look for lost relatives and friends and to find out what had happened to places and property. I think that for them, who had after all been in their forties when they left the country, it was a kind of homecoming; there was so much to which they could still relate. Yet even they never remotely contemplated returning there to live.

In 1952 I spent a few days over the workers' May Day rallies and festivities in Stuttgart and Frankfurt with my natural father, Hans Gottfurcht, I found myself in the company of German socialists who had either been in concentration camps and miraculously survived or had recently returned from exile to help rebuild the labour and trade union movement of their country. I have to confess that I not only enjoyed the

33

company of these people but, despite the widespread devastation and hardship, I liked the ambience  - the cafés and pubs, the scenery , the shops, and I had forgotten how much I liked German food!

The trip did nothing to overcome my basic antagonism, my suspicion of Germans and all things German. But it also left me with a growing curiosity to see again the scenes of my childhood, as well as a desire to meet up with two cousins who had been there throughout. It was not until 1961, twenty-eight years after leaving Berlin that I went back for a week. I sometimes wish I could say that the visit left me cold. It didn't.

The first thing that struck me was that I knew exactly where I was. I left my hotel on the first evening and walked to all the places associated with my previous life there. I went to the corner where our block of flats had stood and since been bombed, and where there were now a few shops and office buildings. Then I walked to the totally unchanged house where my grandparents had lived, and finally around the whole of the district to the former homes of all my relations, many of whom were long dead. I felt a stranger in a foreign city and yet I felt at home, and I am not able to explain that paradox to others.

In visiting all the sights of the city, I renewed a familiarity that I had not expected to experience. This familiarity has grown on many subsequent visits yet without diminishing the sense that I do not belong and my total assurance of being at home in England. I made many trips to the other side of the wall, while it stood, and found myself rather more comfortable in the company of the East Berliners than in the smug affluence in the West of the City; nor did I ever experience any of the check-point unpleasantness which forms such a central part of anti-communist folklore. One cannot condone some of the conduct of the regime in the former German Democratic Republic or forget the atrocities committed by the notorious Stasi - the secret police. The West must, however, learn that not everything was rotten in communist societies and that we do not enhance the cause of democracy by hyperbolic propaganda.

The other ingredient in this strange dichotomy is language. I suppose my precious interest in words gave me a slightly larger vocabulary than usual for a ten year-old. For most of the twenty-eight years after I left Berlin I had heard German at home, but almost fanatically not spoken it. Yet in 1961 I found that I am completely bilingual. This is a very strange phenomenon, best illustrated by an event six years later. I was invited to go to Berlin in 1967 to introduce concepts of group dynamics to some teachers, social workers and psychologists. For a week they spoke to each other in a group and I, in the manner of such seminars, observed and noted their every word. When I got back to London, I showed my notebook to Diane as a joke because she knows no German. We were amazed that, without realising it, I had written every word in English, although only German had been spoken. Yet I had been convinced that I had written exactly what I heard. In certain situations, to be bi-lingual is to live in a strange no-man's land.

My residual Berlin-ness is, however, more than linguistic. I cannot deny that I feel an identity with the whole ethos and idiom of the place. I could not and would not live there and I cannot forget its awful history when I am there. But my visits are different from those to any other city in the world. Reluctantly, British as I am, Londoner as I consider myself to be, I am a Berliner.

# III

## A NON JEWISH JEW

### "German Jews Weren't Jews"

From earliest childhood I had no more than the vaguest of notions that I was Jewish. Nowadays it is difficult for people to appreciate the extent of 'assimilation' of German Jews, especially after the First World War, into the social, cultural and business life of the German community.

My grandparent's generation of Jews in Germany were mostly the children of the first immigrants from further East - from Poland or the 'Polish Corridor', Danzig (Gdansk) and the like, - or from Russia and the Baltic states of Latvia and Lithuania. Others had themselves come from such places - some maintained religious observances. My Helft grandmother still kept the Friday night Sabbath rituals. Yet by no means had all of these grandparents darkened the doors of a synagogue. If they did, it was at the Jewish New Year or on *Yom Kippur*, the Day of Atonement. They were the descendants of *pogrom* victims in Eastern Europe in the 19th century and they kept some of the traditions alive because they had grown up in them. Their Jewish identity was, for them, never in doubt.

I have no recollection that my parents ever went near a synagogue except on one occasion for a relative's wedding. Their generation was 'modern' and shared the frivolities of 1920's Berlin, considering themselves to be sophisticated young Germans. They had been children in the 'Naughty Nineties', they had experienced the Great War and the post-war German Revolution, the abdication if the Kaiser, the indignation at the Versailles

37

peace settlement, the birth of the Weimar Republic, and the slightly phoney between-wars affluence. They were writers and journalists, musicians, actors, film makers and the new broadcasters. They were lawyers and, to a much lesser extent, teachers and social workers. They were businessmen and entrepreneurs. They held posts in all the occupations of the professional and middle classes and saw no difference between themselves and any other Germans of their time. They enjoyed the same café society, the same boom of theatre, music and art. Like their non-Jewish friends and colleagues, they did not suffer particularly from the dreadful unemployment and poverty of the many less fortunate Germans that surrounded them. They had, of course, been frightened by the Great Inflation and some of them were badly, but few terminally, damaged in the 1929 bank crash.

Very many of my parents' friends were left wing in their politics, although my father was, and remained for the rest of his life, a well meaning conservative of the kind that would now be described as 'wet'. He had his own business and worked hard, was a good employer and was well liked by everyone. My mother was the more dominant partner, being an activist in all kinds of fields long before women were expected to involve themselves in such matters. In the 1914-18 war, she had worked as a volunteer with a group of women who ameliorated the conditions of British prisoners of war in a camp on the Berlin racecourse of Ruhleben. She was a member of the Social Democrat Party (SDP). Her brother, Hans (my birth father), was a full-time trade union official and her other brother was a writer.

## A Marxist Schooling

It is therefore not all together surprising that, when it was time for me to start school in 1928, I was sent to the *Weltliche Schule*, the 'secular school'. Of course, in Germany most schools were secular. The secularism of this particular school took the form of teaching in an ethos of conscious humanism and Marxist ideology. To that extent it would be more accurate to describe it as a denominational school. It was situated in the appropriately named Pestalozzi Strasse in Charlottenburg, five minutes' walk from where we lived. Having subsequently attended, taught in or been head of many other schools, I cannot recall ever being happier in a school, or more totally at ease with what it was about, than at the *Weltliche Schule*. Nor do I believe that I am seeing this part of my childhood through rose coloured spectacles.

The school gave us an excellent grounding in basic skills. But it did much more. Through the lively mind and warm personality of Herr Kühl, my class teacher throughout my five years there, I was enabled to develop a keen interest in the world, in history and politics and in society. While I recall no aggressive anti-religious teaching, the underlying principles were of course atheist, and I realised later that we were given a Marxist view of history. Some may say we were brainwashed, but I do not think that is an accurate description of the altogether benign influence of the place. Certainly we all became politically and socially aware at an unusually early age. Herr Kühl and the whole school also fostered in very young children an exceptional awareness of relationships. Our bonds of friendship, to be cruelly severed by what was to befall us, were strong and deep-felt. Through the school my social contacts were much wider than had been enjoyed by my parents, or indeed my contemporaries at more traditional schools. My best friend, Hermann Hans, came from a very deprived family and his only decent meals in those times of hardship were often at our home. His unemployed father also became a regular visitor and friend of my mother's.

I last saw Hermann in 1946, when he visited us in London after his release from a German Prisoner of War camp in Scotland, and I did not treat him well. I had only recently learnt of my grandfather's murder by the Nazis, and of other outrages suffered by members of the family who had stayed in Germany; I was going through a period of believing all Germans were evil. I bitterly regret that I showed no interest in the hardships Hermann himself must have suffered since I had last seen him thirteen years earlier, nor much pleasure at seeing him. He had been a kind and caring boy, a young socialist with me, and he bore much greater scars of deprivation and war service than I would ever know. Whilst there is no excuse for all those who participated willingly in the committal of unspeakable atrocities, the majority of young Germans, like my friend, had little choice but to be enlisted in their country's armed forces. He had clearly looked forward to our reunion and did not deserve my coldness. I have tried to find him since and my inability to do so in the last sixty years continues to make me sad and ashamed. As children he and I were very fond of each other. What a disappointment my cruelty must have been to him.

**Suddenly I'm a Jew**

That then is the background to my sense of non-Jewishness. From the beginning of Nazi propaganda in the early 30's I had been aware that my family would be at risk if Hitler seized power, but I had seen it as a political threat, not a racial one. I had simply not identified with Judaism and it seemed somewhat unreal to me, when it happened, that all the adults in my family were suddenly deemed to be members of a community with which I had not seen them have any contact. It is true that many of their friends were also of Jewish origin, but they seemed to be friends due to common interests rather than for reasons of race or shared religious conviction.

Yet now there emerged this new identity, this new sense of association with other 'Jews'. I say 'Jews' in quotes, because the Jewish shopkeeper across the road whose windows were smashed, the Jewish acquaintance whose husband disappeared, the Jewish relative who lost her job, were nearly all as fundamentally un-Jewish as we were. They too had not observed any religious duties and had not primarily thought of themselves as Jews. Of course there were Jews in Berlin who were religious, who practised their religion and kept its dietary and other laws, but I just had not had any real contact with them.

Now we were to leave the place in which I had spent the first ten years of my life, the place I knew as home. We were to leave so many friends and relations and go to a strange country, all because we were suddenly something I had not really known we were. The months before we left Berlin were a kind of limbo existence. The transfer age to secondary education was ten and the school year began at Easter. So, that April I had to start at the *Gymnasium,* Boy's Grammar School, on the Savigny Platz, which other male members of the family had attended. It was a very far cry from the five happy years I had spent at the *Weltliche Schule* which, in any case, was closed down almost at once by the Nazis. The secondary school

41

was very traditional and stuffily formal. Its academic staff, with their silly Germanic obsession with ranks and titles, were vying with each other to ingratiate themselves with the new regime; the school was a hotbed for early Nazism and anti-Semitism was rife. I knew we were emigrating and that my time at the school would be short, but at the age of ten even a short time lasts forever when you are bullied by adults and peers alike and very unhappy. In a way, the awfulness of the *Gymnasium*, with its nationalistic assemblies, its swastika badges, its baiting of Jews and Socialists, made me look forward to leaving the country, taking away some of the sadness and apprehension. I suppose my time there was worse because at ten one has not yet learned the value of keeping one's mouth shut when it is sensible to do so. Some feel that this is a lesson I did not master in adult life either.

Sometimes when I am asked what I admire about England, my country of adoption, I think about the ugly atmosphere in that Berlin Grammar School in contrast to the tolerance and acceptance I found from staff and contemporaries at school in London.

Our actual emigration from Germany, when it finally came in July 1933, was un-dramatic and unlike the common perception of 'flight'. It was more like going on a summer holiday, although it had been preceded by packing everything up, shipping what one dared under the circumstances, and, of course, some rather awful rounds of goodbyes. My grandfather was devastated and his sadness on the day we left has always stayed with me, as I have already said. At ten I was aware of a great wrench, but not perhaps of the finality.

Our first stop was a three day visit to a relative in the industrial city of Duisburg, where I felt very ill at ease and anxious to get on with what I knew to be a fateful step. If we have to go to England, I thought, let's get on with it. However, we then spent almost a week in the Dutch seaside town of Vlissingen (Flushing) to meet up with my father's brother who was already living in Holland. On our journey out of Germany the train was stopped before the Dutch frontier and Nazi guards took everyone who seemed to be leaving the country permanently into compartments in the last carriage, where we were all strip searched and the adults interrogated. It was frightening and unpleasant, but they did let us go and I still remember feeling the significance of arriving at the Dutch border station. Those who left Germany later in the 30s had to do so much more covertly and in far greater danger. Many, of course, did not make it.

Finally we arrived in England, in the bleak port of Harwich, in the early morning of the 7th August 1933. The chief clerk of a chartered accountant, Mark Banus, whom my father had got to know when he served his apprenticeship in London many years earlier, met our train at Liverpool Street Station. He took us to the station buffet where I asked for sausages and suffered the first disappointment of immigration. British 'bangers' were very different from my favourite snack, the Frankfurter! We were then taken to the Banus home in Willesden Green, in north-west London. There were three daughters, the middle one being my age, and a housekeeper. Mr Banus had been widowed a year or so before. We stayed there for several weeks whilst my father started to pick up his business contacts and tried to establish a niche for himself. Meanwhile we looked for somewhere to live, which in the event was to be in the same district. Money was very tight, for the first time in my life.

My abiding memory of the stay with the Banus family is of the occasion when the housekeeper asked my mother, as we were going out, to get her some Bird's custard powder. This was for us a totally unfamiliar item and my mother's limited English led her to think we should try a pet shop! Unsurprisingly, our request was greeted with some surprise.

From the moment we set foot on English soil we had become 'Jewish refugees'; both these words seemed profoundly odd to me. British Jews felt a great deal of responsibility for, and sympathy with, those who had fled from Nazi Germany. In many cases this gradually turned to impatience and irritation when they found how un-Jewish so many of us were. It was not long before some of them suggested that we had brought it all on ourselves by our wonton assimilation as Germans and our neglect of our faith. Nonetheless, I, who had never been a Jew other than in the eyes of Hitler and all the Nazis at the Berlin grammar school, was now clearly identified as one by Jews and gentiles alike.

On arriving in England I did not possess a word of English; I felt very vulnerable when my mother decided I should go to the local elementary school, Mora Road, where no one spoke anything but English. It was a tough regime. If you didn't know the tables that had been set the previous day you were caned on the hand. Such physical attacks on children by teachers were a barbarity peculiar to the British system of education, with which I never came to terms as pupil or teacher. It was totally degrading for the child and even more so for the teacher administering it; by and large it was an ineffective form of punishment and it was abolished in state education much later than it should have been. I did not tolerate it in either of the schools of which I became the Head. At Mora Road I learnt within a couple of weeks to recite by heart the whole of Stevenson's poem, *The Brook*, without understanding a single word. The wretched refrain 'Men may come and men may go but I go on forever' has stayed with me for the last seventy-nine years. No doubt proponents of corporal punishment would say that this proves its effectiveness. Yet at Mora Road I also encountered the inherent decency and tolerance of the English. I was helped by several teachers who showed real concern for my linguistic isolation and I was accepted rather astonishingly warmly by the other boys. I have pleasant recollections of friendships and not ever having been bullied or made fun of. One (non-Jewish) boy showed me particular kindness and I was privileged to make the speech at his 90th birthday recently – a Mora Road friendship that has lasted longer than either of us could have imagined!

I was monopolised by the Jewish boys, and there were a lot of them in North West London. As I began to be able to communicate, I astonished them with my ignorance of Jewish custom and observance, some of them adopted the tutting disapproval of their parents towards the un-Jewishness of these aliens from Germany. However, they also learned from their parents a sense of obligation, of protectiveness, to the 'refugees'. In retrospect I have always felt that they were very kind to me and, strange as I found some of their ways, I valued their friendship and their efforts to make me feel at home. Their tolerance of an odd contemporary from another world was, I have since felt, incredibly mature.

These were difficult years. I was 'homesick' at first, although it quickly became less clear just where home was. Yet I did miss the surroundings in which I had had a secure childhood and the people who had made it so. Especially I missed my grandfather.

Some children are lucky enough to have one adult with whom they have a specially close and loving rapport; in my case it was my grandfather. It was only later that I understood how very much I am like him, not least in the shortcomings I seem to have inherited - my impatience with those whose views I cannot share, my obsession with punctuality, and other faults which even now I have no wish to make public to those who do not know them. I hope I may have inherited some of his many strengths too.

**Spiritual awakenings**

Before describing my further spiritual development, I must say that I do not believe that my 'spirituality' began when I developed an interest in traditional religions. There was something profoundly spiritual, in the very best sense of the word, in all I had seen in, and learnt from, people who would deny the existence of God. To those who cannot understand that paradox I can only suggest the old, rather childish analogy which they might accept: that if you close your eyes, you can still be seen; if you say you do not believe in God, he is still there. Equally, I believe, if you do not speak of soul and spirit but strive for what is good, if you give priority in your life to values like kindness, compassion and love, you are being spiritual. Some Christians would claim that this is not spirituality at all. Yet these are the qualities I encountered in my school teacher Herr Kühl and his colleagues, amongst many others later on, who were communists or humanists, and did not affirm a religious faith. Christians who are socialists find it self-evident that this is the political system most nearly reflecting the teachings of Jesus. They must not be allowed to think that they have the monopoly in such ideals.

After Mora Road school I was fortunate enough to be admitted to Kilburn Grammar School. Here I continued to be typecast as the German Jew, but was probably the only Jewish boy who had mostly non-Jewish friends. I still could not see that Jewishness was of itself a primary reason for anything, and certainly not a basis for relationships. I have continued to believe the less religious a Jew is, the more his self-conscious affirmation of his origin is a racial matter and therefore as irrelevant, even undesirable, as any other form of racialism.

There is, of course, the concept of a Jewish nation. This clearly has historical and biblical significance, but I have never found its modern application convincing. I totally understand that those who have survived terrible suffering in the holocaust, and in other persecutions, are entitled to a place where they can make a new life. To this extent there is cause for a Jewish 'homeland'. That, however, is surely a matter of politics and social organisation rather than of nationality and race; it does not excuse imperialism or the persecution of others who have lived in the same region for centuries by those who themselves have been persecuted. Old Testament teaching about *diaspora* and the Israelites' homeland merits fuller discussion than is appropriate here.

Nor is it easy to justify the religious intolerance shown by a minority of Israelis with political 'king making' power, to their less religious compatriots. Not so long ago, the son of a cousin of mine had to travel to Cyprus with his fiancée for the civil solemnisation of their marriage, because a non-religious ceremony was not available to them in their own country, Israel.

Kilburn Grammar School, in the then Borough of Willesden, served an area of North West London in which very many Jewish people lived. There were a considerable number of Jewish boys at the school and, indeed, among its most able pupils. I valued the friendship of some of them very greatly and through it gained an entrée into their homes and social circle. Their observance of their religion, with its Sabbath routines and its regular attendance at what they called synagogue, came to fascinate me and I started to put in occasional appearances. There was a fairly charismatic rabbi at the synagogue in Cricklewood and I engaged in several discussions with him. I think I quite enjoyed the services; I learnt some Hebrew and became involved in a culture that was entirely new to me. Yet I had reservations not only about any sort of personal faith, but also about aspects of the teaching, reservations which I only began to understand more fully when I became a Christian several years later.

There was also considerable tension for me between this new-found interest, I can describe it as no stronger than an interest, and my unchanging political convictions and ideals. London suburban Jewry in the 1930s was very middle class, very comfortable, very inward looking and self-sufficient. Many were first generation 'immigrants' to suburbia from the East End, where their parents and grandparents had settled on arrival from Eastern Europe. It was the personification of bourgeoisie, a slightly *'nouveau' bourgeoisie*. Of course, my own life had never been exactly proletarian, but my friendships had been, and my concerns had centred on the conditions of the less privileged and the system which create such inequalities.

So I fluctuated between attending the synagogue in Walm Lane and the communist party headquarters in King Street, meeting more interesting people and, sometimes, to watch films like *Potemkin*, which at that time was in a grey area of legality. My life was of course primarily focussed upon school. As my English became more fluent and accent free I took part in many school activities, especially the debating society, where I was often called upon, for some reason, to speak for the more radical motions or against the establishment.

Perhaps here I should make it clear that I did not pursue only serious interests in my teens. In those days we were called 'adolescents' not teenagers and I fully indulged in all the interests and behavioural excesses associated with that age group. This is the place for me to note that it is often said that sex and sexuality were invented in the 60's, the time of the Beatles and the Rolling Stones. They weren't!

My relationship with my parents was not good in those years, partly because I was fed up with being a 'foreigner' and they could, of course, at their age, probably never conceive of themselves as being anything else. So I began to refuse to speak German at home and persisted with this into adult life. I am not proud of my arrogant behaviour towards them and can only plead that it was not easy for me to become a full member of the society into which I had been transplanted whilst finding at home constant reminders of an alien background. Yet it has to be said, to my parents my behaviour was that of a horrid adolescent!

# IV
## MEETING CHRISTIANITY

When I was in the Lower Fifth form (now Year 10) a new master joined the staff at Kilburn Grammar to teach Classics and Religious Education. It was assumed that I had opted out of the latter subject with all the other Jewish boys on religious grounds. In fact I had persuaded my parents to withdraw me from the lessons; I considered myself an atheist. The new teacher, Don Woodman, had been Head Boy of the school a few years previously and this was his second post since graduating. To say that he was a man of strong personality would be an understatement. He immediately gave enormous life and interest to our Latin and Greek lessons. His teaching style simply bubbled over with his own enthusiasm for his subject. I can still recite chunks of Latin and Greek from the classics he taught us. He took over the school dramatic society and involved himself in every aspect of school life. It became known that he was motivated by his strong Christian faith and church membership. Don was a firm disciplinarian and had a rather unhealthy liking for punishing boys by hitting their backsides with a slipper, but he at least knew his pupils and took a close interest in them. We soon clashed at a school debate in which I insensitively attacked his religious convictions.

My Sixth Form life began on 1$^{st}$ September 1939. Schools had been ordered to return early from the long holiday and we were all bidden to attend with suitcases packed with basic belongings. My first job as Sub-Prefect at that stage was to distribute labels and name tags to the forms allocated to me and we then marched those who were present to Queens Park station further down Salusbury Road. Of course some parents had opted to keep their sons in London so the school was a little depleted for the evacuation. The Head, apparently unbeknown to his staff or authority, had enlisted in the Royal Army Education Corpse, and we were under the leadership of the Senior Master, 'Jock' Westbury but somewhere after we all left Queens Park, he and a group of pupils got detached from the main party and ended up in Market Harborough while the rest of the school arrived in Northampton.

We were taken to a reception centre and allocated to billets in a scene reminiscent of a cattle market! 'I want that little blonde one' a woman would say while another shouted out that she didn't want any boy over 13. The history of the war has not given enough credit to the families in places like Northampton who opened their homes to children from the big cities with very varying backgrounds, often homesick and quite unprepared for the challenges of fitting into the home of strangers. There were tensions, some inappropriate behaviour by both hosts and evacuees, but on the whole the people of Northampton offered generous hospitality, affection and tolerance. But what a burden these people took upon themselves. I myself landed up with a young married couple. The husband was not conscripted because he worked in a 'reserve occupation' – a factory in his case, manufacturing something vital for the war effort. What were they to make of this young stranger with a foreign name and from they-knew-not-where! My first faux pas was to sit on a chair which I was told was 'Sally's chair'. Sally turned out to be a huge Irish red setter that ruled the house and took some time to accept the stranger. Her owners could not have been kinder or more hospitable.

We had half day lessons in the buildings which we shared with the Northampton Town and County (later Northampton Grammar) School. Don Woodman persuaded Willesden Education Committee to acquire a three-story terraced property in Kingsthorpe Road, to be called Youth House, where he would live as resident warden. It was furnished as a youth centre, not only for Kilburn Grammar but also for the pupils from the other evacuated secondary schools from Willesden. The youth centre housed recreational facilities and became a place where the evacuees could pursue private study during those parts of the day in which the school was not available to them. Escaping from our billets and our reluctant hosts was a priority for many of us and Youth House was a real haven. It would not have been so without Don's personality and leadership.

When he astounded me by inviting me to live there as his Assistant Warden he must have known it would adversely affect my studies, and I certainly did not, in the event, do as well as I should have done in my Higher School Certificate - the forerunner of A-levels. Moving to Youth House was, however, to change my life. For a long time I had had much to say, not least to Woodman, about serving the community. Here was a practical opportunity for me to put my words into action. However, as we worked together, it was he who was successful and I who struggled with the day to day practical and human relationship problems that arose.

One night I walked into his room to discuss some minor organisational matter and found him on his knees, saying his prayers. I had vaguely heard that some people did this sort of thing, but I had thought it unlikely. Neither of us could ignore my intrusion and we began that evening a process of discussion which was to continue for nearly a year, until he joined the Navy. Our discussion gradually evolved and became less debate and more instruction as time went by. After a while, rather as I had flirted with Jewish worship two or three years earlier, I began to disappear on a Sunday morning or evening, not telling anyone that I was exploring the worship of local churches.

When describing a religious conversion, it is difficult to distinguish between the emotional and that which is strictly cerebral. Any shining light on our individual roads to Damascus, like St Paul, is surely usually a mixture of mind and feeling, and it is impossible for us to discern the levels of divine intervention. My acceptance of the existence of God, of Christian teaching and of a personal Saviour was slow, very gradual and involved much mental anguish. It has made me suspicious of those evangelists, like Billy Graham, who would lead great masses of people to dramatic experiences and instant conversion. It is not for us to say that God cannot or does not work like that. However, I am glad that He chose not to change my life in that fashion. For me there was no sudden blinding light and I believe I am expected to use my brain to consider Christian teaching and practice in ways that make sense to me.

Jesus welcomed 'little children' and this is probably taken as acceptance of child-like faith. Those who can achieve it are perhaps to be envied. To those of us who can only come to Christianity as adults it is a wonder how, for example, water from some 'shrine' can be thought to have miraculous powers; or that certain aspects of Maryology are anything more than superstition.

I found no conflict between my new-found Christianity and my socialism. Rather, they enlightened each other. As I grew more acquainted with various forms of worship, the concept of the Christian community became increasingly important to me. It seemed to me, right from the start, that unless Christianity is expressed in society it is quite meaningless. Christ's teaching about what is meant by loving our neighbour is unequivocal and leaves no room for the ordinary Christian to be a hermit or to seek membership in inward looking holy huddles. I am here, of course, not dismissing vocations to the religious life; indeed, most such vocations are far from being calls to ignore the world, but rather to support its needs in a special way.

I knew, at this stage, far too little to form any theological judgements about the various denominations. I suppose I initially thought of myself as an Anglican largely because Don Woodman was one, though he seemed fairly far out at the Protestant wing of the Church of England and might have been content for me to join one of the non-conformist churches. I did find, as I moved around the churches in Northampton, that I was aesthetically more comfortable with the form of worship in the parish church than anywhere else. The matter was probably clinched for me one Sunday evening when, late in 1940, I heard at St. Giles, the church in Northampton town centre, a preacher from the Industrial Christian Fellowship. He was putting into words all I was beginning to feel about the social implications of Christianity. He gave a vivid account of a factory entirely devoted to making wooden pips for imitation fruit jams!

In retrospect it seems absurd that within a few months of my starting on this pilgrimage I was being asked by Don to conduct or speak at the regular

Youth House Sunday evening services. I cannot judge whether I did anything for those who came; we certainly got very good attendances. For me it was an enormous help to have to think about my new religion at this level. It also may have been the catalyst for my vocation – a growing sense that the only way for me to make real sense of what I had found was to spend my life in its service, its ministry. At this stage, however, I still believed that I would be a school teacher, as I had hoped from earliest childhood. I am so lucky that I was in fact going to be allowed to combine both vocations.

A link was forged between those leaving school and returning to North West London from Northampton and St. Catherine's, the parish church of Neasden. The young vicar, Charles Crowson, (known for some reason at that time by his middle name of Sidney) was a man of outstanding drive and personality and a brilliant preacher. Nowadays he would be called a workaholic. Neither he nor his curates had a formal 'day off' throughout the war. His wife and children were evacuated and he lived in the Vestry after the vicarage was bombed, active in the service of his parish from early morning to the end of his fire watching shift late into the night. St. Catherine's had, even for those days, huge congregations and flourishing social activities, especially for young people. A thriving youth club in the church hall was always open as its name, the Monday to Friday Club, implies and it had flourishing junior boys' and junior girls' sections. Crowson's vestry became very much a home from home for a group of us and our discussions and planning went long into the air raid nights.

For me this was a time of many disparate but simultaneous activities. Though still unqualified, I was very fortunate to obtain a teaching post at

Leopold Road Secondary School in a fairly tough area of Willesden. It was, of course, before the Butler Act, so the school was still an 'elementary' but the Head who was, to say the least, eccentric, was a brilliant teacher and I look back on the period at Leopold Road as a wonderful apprenticeship. Such 'student teacher appointments' were not unusual in those days.

Perhaps Reg Holloway merits a paragraph to himself. He stamped his eccentric personality on every part of the school. The hall had 382 little 'v's painted on the floor for 382 pairs of heels of the pupils! Staff stood on either side of the small platform facing the pupils. Reg reigned supreme - never without a punishment cane in his hand - and with it he beat time to the hymn and then to the pauses he wanted kept between the clauses of the Lord's Prayer. During the hymn he shouted 'BREATH!' at appropriate moments and he contrived to stand in front of any teacher who had slipped in a moment or two late to shout at them 'the beginning of this day' when he came to those words in the morning prayer. During the rest of the day he was liable to burst into any classroom, stick still in hand, yell 'five sevens, three eights, none of them know their tables!' and storm out again. On the other hand he would come into the classroom of a young, inexperienced teacher like myself, say 'go and sit at the back somewhere' and proceed to give a model lesson of huge skill, with the children lapping it up and participating. I learned an enormous amount from him but I don't think I would have wanted to take some of his odd leadership methods into my own headships! What would Ofsted make of him today? In some ways he was so bonkers that he might have got on well with Michael Gove. All in all however, Leopold Road was a wonderful induction into the teaching profession and I owe much to the colleagues there who accepted and mentored me.

To some extent this teaching post was seen by the powers-that-be to serve also as a cover job for a rather strange form of war service that relied on my bi-lingual ability and which, by its nature, had to be part time and secret. At the same time I began external study for my London University Degree. I became involved in the youth work at St.Catherine's and took over the junior boys section, and then the conduct of the Junior Church on Sundays after the curate, Ray Bowers, joined the army as a chaplain.

In a very short space of time I had met Christianity, explored it, committed myself to it and was spending much of my time actively engaged in it.

# V

## FINDING A THEOLOGY

St. Catherine's was very much in the evangelical tradition. Charles Crowson had been a curate in Crouch End of the well known Canon Brian Green and was steeped in the whole of what was called the 'Green Line' approach of missions and conversions, and challenging sermons. Green was by this time vicar of Holy Trinity, Brompton Road, and I sometimes went there to hear him. He was certainly charismatic, but I wonder whether he would altogether approve of the extremes to which that church and many like it have more recently moved.

Crowson without doubt exercised more influence on my life than anyone else at that stage and greatly affected very many young, and for that matter not so young, people who attended St.Catherine's and its various organisations at the time. I owe much to him and, although I have moved a long way from his tradition, I learnt a lot that has stayed with me. He was a good friend and mentor and he did much to foster and interpret my vocation, leading me first through Baptism and Confirmation, against bitter protest from my parents. I shall always be grateful for the way he enriched my life. We frequently clashed, not least because he resented it when any of his protégés made choices that were not entirely in keeping with his advice.

I think I first became aware of a difference of interpretation when we were all excited and inspired by the Archbishop of Canterbury, William Temple's, motivating leadership. Temple proclaimed a church which 'is the only organisation that exists primarily for those who do not belong to it'. To evangelicals like Crowson this was primarily a call to evangelism. I saw it more as a call to the church to serve the community; a summons to perpetuate Christ's ministry to those whom others find it hard to love.

One of the leading lay people at St.Catherine's was Leslie Corry, who in his own way also greatly influenced the younger generation. He was a bachelor, who devoted much time to introducing us to theatre, concerts and choral services at places like Westminster Abbey and visits to such disparate places of worship as All Saints', Margaret Street and All Souls, Langham Place, not to mention the joys of pub crawling! Leslie was an altogether civilising influence and a very good friend in good times and in bad for many years. He became one of the godfathers of our younger son, Peter, and died in 1966. No record of my life and those who had a part in shaping it would be complete without a tribute to Leslie.

Because he tended to see it in terms of practices rather than theology, it was difficult to explain to Charles Crowson how I was being drawn to the more Catholic tradition of anglicanism. I had, just before the end of the war, been appointed to a teaching post at the King's School, Ely, and so had become acquainted with the theological college there. Its worship and quiet discipline appealed greatly to me. At the same time I was learning of the work of the great Anglo-catholic priests in the East End of London since the second part of the 19th century. They seemed to me to have brought the Gospel to deprived sections of society in a particularly relevant way and their form of liturgy introduced colour and excitement to those living drab and sometimes hopeless lives. I began to understand the richness of sacramentalism and to see a historical perspective that I felt had perhaps been missing in the evangelical tradition, through which I had come to Christianity and to which I will always acknowledge my indebtedness. It is also the historical perspective that most nearly reconciled for me at that stage the tensions between Christianity and the Marxist background from which I came.

At the same time I found out about the early Christian socialists: Bishop Gore, Henry Scott Holland, R.H. Tawney and the others of their generation, some of whom were involved in the Christian Social Union of the late 19$^{th}$ and early 20$^{th}$ century. Later I was to meet and work alongside their successors - such men as Stanley Evans and Edward Charles, and of course quite especially Donald Soper- in the Christian Socialist Movement. My new theology was taking shape. So I withdrew from the offer of a place at Ridley Hall, Cambridge, and began my training at Ely Theological College in September 1946.

**Becoming a priest**

Anglican training of ordinands has strengths and weaknesses and there have been enormous changes in the decades since I was ordained. In that context, Ely had many faults but far more good points. The Principal was Canon Henry Balmforth, who had been a public school headmaster and was a theologian of some renown. His works, especially his commentaries on St. Luke's Gospel, are still used. He had wide interests and a genuine concern for the 'young men' of his college. He was also a snob, who regularly humiliated before distinguished guests those of us whose degrees were not Oxbridge. On the other hand, he tolerated my starting a college Labour Party branch, when he could, of course, have prevented my doing so. It was the time of the Atlee government's greatest successes and he was

60

no doubt wise enough to know that I would have much support in the college. He insisted on being known and addressed by the quaint title of 'Princeps'.

Balmforth's health was indifferent and he had to take a term's sick leave during which we had the enormous good fortune of the college being led by Michael Ramsey, at that time still Regius Professor at Cambridge. I was to have the privilege of his interested patronage again years later, when I was head of a school virtually next to Lambeth Palace. His lectures at Ely on Hebrews and on eschatology, and his general influence during the term he visited the college, were intellectually the highlight of my time there.

The other significant influence at Ely was the Vice Principal, Robert Daubney. He introduced me to writers like Barth on the one hand, and Reinhold Niebuhr on the other, giving breadth to my rather immature understanding of theological thought. Robert also put things into context for me by his love of church history. He was involved in the Christendom movement and I attended a number of their meetings with him, coming across many interesting people, though I was never totally comfortable with their somewhat laid back academic approach to matters which seemed to me to require action more than words. Robert shared my somewhat iconoclastic attitudes and remained a friend, becoming another of Peter's godfathers.

The previous ten years had been really rather hectic. Ely was for me above all, the chance to take a deep breath and relax; the opportunity to learn prayer, meditation and worship; a time to formulate and organise the jumble of ideas and ideals which had brought me to this point and to have light shed on them by those under whom I had placed myself.

Some of the discipline of the college was irksome, yet I knew it was what I needed at that time. The routine of the daily Offices – from Prime and Matins to Compline - the time set aside for meditation in the chapel each day and, above all, of course, the place of the daily Mass and the meticulous care with which the liturgy was carried out – all these things nourished a hunger in me which I had up to that point not really had time to perceive. To learn to serve in the Sanctuary at Mass was a greatly valued new experience for me whereas the other students had of course grown up with such practices.

In later life I regret very much that I have not used the opportunities at various times to be more 'academic'. I have always been torn between my deep interest in the 'why' and the urgency of 'how'. My impatience has tended to let the practical prevail over the theory which undergirds it, and I think I am probably in many ways the poorer for it.

All my generation of ordinands came to their training from some form of hectic activity, mainly in active war service. Most of us had held some kind of positions of authority and, unlike our predecessors, did not come to theological college straight from school or university. Our needs and experience were different from those who were ordained pre-war, and the college did not always find it easy to adapt. Yet Ely, although so steeped in tradition, grasped this nettle with surprising courage and did remarkably well by us, though some of my contemporaries will be surprised to find me expressing such tolerant sentiments with the benefit of hindsight!

# VI

## ORDINATION AND MINISTRY

I remember a conversation at dinner in college one night of a group of us, the Principal and a rather pompous Bishop. The talk turned to 'specialist ministries' and the Bishop asked one of my friends whether he felt called to a specialism. "Yes, my Lord," he said, "the episcopate"! At that time I still felt - indeed have continued to feel- great surprise that I was called to the priesthood at all, but I already had grave doubts whether I would be of much use in a parochial ministry. I wanted to find a way of combining my love of schools, education and my interest in young people with my ministry.

I was becoming increasingly interested in the treatment of juvenile delinquency and asked the Home Office for permission to visit an Approved School. They sent a list and I chose one in Chelmsford on the somewhat bizarre grounds that the Head was one of the few listed who did not have an O.B.E. After a preliminary visit I spent two successive college vacations helping out at the Essex Home School. The Head, Ron Coultard, then asked whether I thought the church would allow me to go there after ordination as chaplain and housemaster. This post would involve responsibility for all out-of-classroom activity and contact with the boys' homes and families, in addition to the boys' general spiritual welfare, religious education and the conduct of worship.

Henry Balmforth, the Principal of Ely Theological College, ('Princeps') was appalled and all these years later I can agree that he had reason to be. I think it was a mistake to work in a situation of abnormality before

63

acquiring some maturity in more normal work. However, I did not see it like that at the time and sought an interview with the Bishop of Chelmsford, Henry Wilson. I have heard people say that Wilson was a bigoted evangelical with barely concealed contempt for those who did not share his views; I know some who actually experienced him in this way. I have to say that I myself found him kind and sympathetic, showing no antagonism to my anglo-catholic churchmanship.

He seemed to understand why I wanted to start my ministry in such an unusual job. Indeed, considering his age and background, he was extremely sensitive to where I had come from and what I felt called to do. It so happened that the parish of the Ascension in which the school was situated had a splendid priest, Ashley Turner, who was well known as a very good training Vicar. To my delight, and Henry Balmforth's dismay, it was eventually arranged that I should serve as Turner's curate in that parish, living and working at the school.

Ordination is an experience that I suppose is almost impossible to describe to lay people. Mine, at Chelmsford Cathedral on 19th September 1948, was the culmination of so much and the end of a long journey; I found it unbelievably moving. I had a strange sense of coming home after a very turbulent voyage and, for all my impatience with much of what the Church of England often says and does, I have never really lost that sense of it being my safe haven. It meant a great deal to me that, despite their strong misgivings about what I was doing, indeed their most vehement opposition to it, my parents felt able to come to the service and to entertain my friends to lunch afterwards.

There was, however, a cloud. A few days before the ordination Ashley Turner was taken ill with tuberculosis and was never to return to the parish. I had lost my training vicar. So during my diaconate I was rather clumsily trying to look after the parish as well as learning my job in the school. A very elderly and frail retired priest had been brought in by the Bishop to maintain the sacramental tradition of the place. Of course, at the age of twenty-five one takes these things in one's stride with the self-assurance of youth but I was glad that my batteries had been fully charged by the previous two years at Ely.

I look back on my Approved School chaplaincy with mixed feelings. The challenge was enormous. The vast majority of the boys had undoubtedly been more sinned against than sinning. They were casualties of society and their vulnerability showed itself in many ways. For example, a quite disproportionate number of these young adolescents were eneuretic ('bed wetters'). Yet, whilst few of them were high flyers, they were by no means all academically backward. As with any causalities, their 'injuries', though mainly emotional, were not always pretty to behold. Some of them had developed very anti-social attitudes and habits. It has to be said that among those who knew well the difference between 'right' and 'wrong' there were those who, in their deliberate choice of wrong, took no account of the damage done to the victims of their offences. A few of them were destined to become life-long criminals whose 'progress' one was able to follow in the newspapers in later years.

The school was small enough (150) for me to get to know all of them and whilst I got close to most of them I cannot claim that all of them responded positively. The regime was tough but not oppressive and, although some of the staff who had worked in that system for many years were slightly cynical, most were dedicated to giving these youngsters some sort of chance in life. Compared to the retributive attitudes of more recent governments, the emphasis in the 1950s was on rehabilitation rather than punishment. In Approved Schools at that time, society was definitely not trying to get its own back on those who had offended and been sent to us by the courts.

I visited all their homes, mostly in the East End of London and the new slums of the Essex marshes, but also in other parts of Essex and the Home Counties. Whilst many were at least superficially well cared for, I saw some quite unspeakable squalor and terrible social, as well as economic, deprivation. Some of the parents were shamefully neglectful and it was clear that none of our efforts would produce stable and supportive homes to which to release their sons. A few, however, were touchingly grateful for what the school was trying to do and to some of them I became a kind of unofficial parish priest. On days when they visited their sons at the school I was often as much in demand to listen to their own problems as other staff were being asked to give information about the boys' progress. My attempts to forge working links with the boys' parish clergy were only very partially successful, although I called on them each time I had to make visits to a home on their patch.

As the chaplain, I found many of the boys receptive and anxious to share their anxieties. We were able to build a chapel and each year I prepared the boys for confirmation. We began to have mid-week as well as Sunday Eucharists and after a while the school enjoyed a very full sacramental life. I was resident in the school and lived a very busy life.

Clergy are, of course, always vulnerable because, rather like doctors, they can do part of their work only in private encounters with one person. Unfortunately a small number of the most damaged of the boys, one of whom I had had reason to punish, took advantage of this and were sufficiently street-wise to put me in a great deal of peril - from which I was very fortunate to be able to extricate myself. Perhaps if I had gone to this job with a little more experience, or I had not lost the benefit of Ashley Turner's supervision, I might have been a little less naive and laid myself less open to the unpleasant accusations that were made. The whole business had led me always to sympathise with people who are accused without any corroborative evidence. I doubt whether in today's climate, with its hysterical witch-hunt of any against whom there is the merest breath of suspicion, I would have been as justly treated.

Overall, however, my time at the Essex Home School was a happy one and I learned much from it and from my colleagues there and in other Approved Schools. I can only hope that I also contributed a little.

The treatment of young offenders is complex and always requires a disproportionate investment of material resources and manpower. In the last twenty years successive governments have tried to do things on the cheap. Worse, they have moved increasingly from explaining to blaming. For all their protestations they singularly neglect to tackle 'the causes of crime' and subscribe to policies of naming and shaming, and to inappropriate imitations of the worst type of American penal institutions, like boot camps. I found, like many of my colleagues in Approved Schools at the time, that it is far from easy to achieve a balance between feeling sorry for the boys because they had been so badly damaged by society and, on the other hand, addressing that damage. Governments have a duty to eliminate the inequalities and deprivations which breed juvenile crime. They then have to put in place structures in which the offenders can be helped to face up to their deviant behaviour and given self-esteem to support their future role in society.

It was wonderful for me that while I was in Chelmsford, Douglas Rhymes was appointed as priest in charge of the Ascension. He shared many of my ideas and ideals, teaching me an enormous amount during the time we worked together. My friendship with him continued throughout his subsequent time in the Southwark diocese and lasted until his death. Douglas was a good priest and a profound thinker. In the latter section of this book in which I deal with the influence of the Sixties, I have referred to some of his writing. I wonder whether the church really used his great pastoral and intellectual gifts as effectively as it might have done.

**In a parish**

After four years I left Chelmsford and went to a curacy in Birmingham, which I enjoyed, but which confirmed my conviction that the parish ministry was not my forte. Holy Cross, Billesley, was at that time a lively parish with a moderate catholic tradition. It served predominantly, though not exclusively, a working class and blue collar community in the southern suburb of the city. Church attendances were excellent in those early days of the 1950's, which saw the Parish and People movement and other similar initiatives. I learnt about parochial worship and organisations and about visiting, which I had never done in that sense before and which does not seem to be practiced in quite the same way nowadays. At the weekly meeting with the vicar I had to produce a list of visits done and visits planned - visits to the sick, to church members, and 'cold' visits in a designated part of the parish. Visiting was not a popular activity among curates, but I was so new to parochial work that I quite enjoyed the huge variety of unexpected situations one would encounter. However, I spent a great proportion of my time in the local State Schools and in parish youth work.

Within less than two months I had done what, at that time, was considered unforgivable. I fell in love with a girl in the parish. The vicar, and particularly the vicar's wife, who were of my own sort of age and whom I had known for some time, did not approve and forbade us to have contact within the parish. Diane was banned from all activities. She had previously run the Cubs and was a Sunday school teacher. Now, suddenly, she was no longer deemed fit to do these things. We were expected only to meet away from Billesley and only on my day off. In fact we usually met at the churchwarden's house and the whole parish was delighted by our happiness. We were married at Holy Cross, by Charles Crowson, just thirteen months after my arrival in the parish, and five years to the day after my ordination. There were so many local people in the church that we still believe that no one would have noticed if we had not turned up. The vicar had gone away when the Banns were due to be read. I had to do so in his absence and asked the congregation that 'if any of you know just cause or impediment... you are to queue up by the vestry after the service'. I have sometimes wondered whether this departure from the legal wording has made our marriage invalid! The sceptical said, 'It won't last'. At the time of writing we have managed 59 years.

## Specialist ministries

Clearly we could not stay in Birmingham once we were married. By a strange series of events and chance encounters I was invited by The Missions to Seamen (now known as the Mission to Seafarers) to go to Japan to rebuild their work in Yokohama and to be Rector of Christ Church, which had been the English speaking church before the war. In the event, because the chaplain of Kobe was requested to leave rather hurriedly, I was asked to take over the mission there first. For a year I began the work in Yokohama by commuting, which in those days took 12 hours by train or involved a quite uncomfortable flight. Nowadays it is about three hours by 'bullet train'. Our three years living in Yokohama, after a new chaplain arrived in Kobe, were more settled. We enjoyed a fascinating four years in Japan, a wonderful start to our married life.

After Japan and a short home leave, we were sent to Port Sudan on the Red Sea, where our stay was very brief. When we got there in June 1957 I read the correspondence between the local committee and Missions to Seamen headquarters in London. The Port Sudan committee wrote three letters, in the first they wrote; 'This is not a good place to which to send a married man'. In their second letter they said, 'Allright, but don't send someone with a child'. Their final message read, 'Whoever you send, don't let them arrive here between May and September, it would kill them'. So, naturally, they sent me and Diane and 22 month old Michael in June! It is not entirely surprising that almost immediately we were all quite ill and that the Bishop in the Sudan, Oliver Allison, sent us back home in August. I can't say we were too sorry. It was an awful place and, of course, long before the days when one could expect any form of air conditioning. We did, however,

70

experience most of the biblical plagues - a sand storm which penetrated even the hermetically sealed fridge, a smallpox epidemic, and in Khartoum the incredible sight of a swarm of locusts and its destruction of all the greenery in sight in mere seconds.

When we returned to London I was appointed Schools and Candidates Secretary at the society's head office with responsibility for the recruitment of chaplains and lay workers. I was also charged with the society's publicity and publications and started a monthly newspaper, *The Flying Angel*, which has only this year been replaced by a publication in a different format.

Essentially the ministry of the church is the same wherever it is exercised. If asked what parochial ministry consists of, the answer would surely be that it meets the needs of all the people in the parish by showing the love of Christ in a number of ways. The priests administer the sacraments and present Christian teaching, and they involve their lay people in being alongside all parishioners in every situation. They perpetuate Christ's ministry of teaching and baptising, healing and forgiving, of breaking bread as a Christian community sacramentally and also socially.

Specialist ministries exist for precisely the same purpose. Just as the emphasis of the work in one parish has to differ in style from that in the neighbouring one, so each non-parochial ministry has to address the special needs of those to whom it is addressed. There is no great mystique in this. It is obvious that the chaplain in a high security men's prison does not have to work out how best to involve his branch of the Mother's Union in the overall strategy of his work. The chaplain in a geriatric hospital does not need to advertise for 'a colleague good with youth'!

So seafarers' chaplains have special opportunities to be alongside those to whom they minister in the world's ports. Sacraments are offered when needed, and not only at set times. The intellectual engagement of Christian seamen and of enquirers alike presents new challenges, but also new opportunities when men spend days, sometimes weeks, at sea. Sick visiting takes on a new urgency when someone is in a hospital thousands of miles away from any of his loved ones. Prison visits are pressing and tend to take on political and diplomatic overtones in some foreign ports. The social activities in which the church acts host to its parishioners are of new importance when the guests are homesick and in a country where they don't speak the language and where the seaman is easy prey to every confidence trickster and tout. The facilities which the church offers these people are different from those needed in a parish at home. There is, for example, generally no need to turn the village telephone into a public utility. In a port, seafarers often want first to phone home and have nowhere to do so but from the seamen's club.

In the work of the Mission to Seafarers the church quite uniquely shows the universality of Christ. Through this society the Anglican Communion works everywhere in the world, alongside colleagues from many other nationalities and denominations, often sharing facilities and ministries with them, and it serves men and women of every race and nation. Before the collapse of the communist regimes in Europe, the Christian ministry to seafarers provided one of the few opportunities for the church to bring together people from both sides of the 'iron curtain'.

With the advent of container ships and the consequent rapid turn round in ports, the work of the Mission to Seafarers has changed enormously since I was involved in it. Hostels, for example, are needed less or in different circumstances. However, the basic function of the work is the same and exactly that of every other ministry of the church. The 'perils of the sea' are as great as ever and seafarers now face deadly danger from the resurgence of piracy, notably in the Indian Ocean area.

Wherever it is at work the Church has always to be sensitive to the social implications of the Gospel. The Mission to Seafarers works alike with ship-owners and seafarers' organisations and unions. Seafarers suffer hardship, indignities and danger through the greed and neglect of some who own ships; and the society has always seen it as its Christian duty to intervene as appropriate whilst retaining the most cordial relationship with the good ship-owners, many of whom in turn support the mission financially and in many other ways.

Is it a Missionary Society? The origin of many Missionary Societies lies in 19th century imperialism, when the church shared the arrogant assumptions of the age and sought to bring the Gospel to what Kipling called the 'lesser breeds without the law'. To some extent seafarers ranked alongside Africans as being in need of paternalistic benefaction; but then so, in a different way, did the slum dwellers in the cities at home. In fact the legend has it that the origin of the society dates back to John Ashley looking at the ships at anchor in the Bristol Channel and his son asking 'How do those men get to church?' The result was that Ashley resolved to take the church to the seafarers. In that sense it is of course still a Missionary Society, but surely no more than every activity of the church. In parish or industry,

73

hospital, school or prison, or in working with a branch of the church overseas, Christian ministry is a mission, being 'sent' to show Christ to the world.

Just as it is to be hoped that no curate would now be treated as I was in Birmingham simply because Diane and I had fallen in love, so too the kind of disciplines applied by the church have generally changed enormously, and for the better. As an outstanding example of what one accepted in 1953 and would not today, I relate the astonishing decision by The Missions to Seamen about our voyage to Japan.

It was felt that I should use the trip - six weeks in a small cargo ship which carried six passengers - to 'learn the ropes' of being a seamen's chaplain. The company of my new wife, it was felt, would be so much of a distraction that she could not be allowed to sail in the same ship! A few weeks before my departure, Diane was summoned all the way to London to be officially 'vetted', without me being allowed to be present, by the Deputy General Secretary, who forgot the appointment. She was then seen by another official and, subsequently, they arranged that she would travel in a similar ship, which would leave England two months after I had sailed in the *m.v. Glengarry*. It was a cruel and needless separation, and particularly heartless because Diane, ten years younger than me and at the tender age of twenty, had hardly left Birmingham, let alone travelled on her own to the other side of the world.

On the night of their departure from Southampton a very homesick Diane was cheered no end by a young ship's officer, who told her that they were in for a terrible voyage because 'we're taking some parson's wife all the way to Japan'! She did not, at this time, inform him that she was the person to which he was referring. At least the captain of her ship, the *m.v. Soudan*, took a paternal interest. He quickly instructed her that at sea, in those days, orange juice, which she had asked for at a party in his cabin, cost 6 old pennies whilst gin was only 2d. Consequently, by the time Diane arrived in Japan, she had acquired one of the more important social habits of the ex-patriot Brit in the Far East. I had meanwhile been taught by the captain of my ship the equally essential skills of the game Liar Dice. I can't think why I was rather good at it!

The Missions to Seamen engendered a very strong bond between those who worked in it. Forty years later, on a visit to our son in Australia, we visited ports there and on stopovers and everywhere were made to feel like returning members of a close knit family by today's chaplains and by the headquarters staff who commended us to them. I have noticed this same sense of belonging among members of other Missionary Societies and among those who share any specialist ministry. When I worked in an Approved School there were few housemasters and fewer chaplains, but when we met we felt a great sense of unity. This sadly does not always seem to be the case in chapters of parochial clergy. I have known chapters in which one got the impression of an element of mutual suspicion and that they almost felt they had to protect their individual empires against each other. Of course others, like the one with which I have been fortunate to be associated in Worcester, are splendidly collegial and collaborative.

# VII

## EAST OF SUEZ

One thinks today of Japan as a major industrial country. However, when we were there in the 1950s, Japan had recently lost the war, suffering enormous physical damage, and had acquired a reputation of unspeakable cruelty in its treatment of prisoners of war. Japan had been a humiliated and underwent a certain 'loss of face', a serious matter to Orientals.

Since the 1945 surrender and the dreadful atomic bomb horrors of Hiroshima and Nagasaki, Japan had been occupied by Americans under the insensitive leadership of General MacArthur, who had arrogated to himself the kind of status previously held by the god-emperor. Traffic in Tokyo was stopped when the General was driven to and from his home at lunch time. Subsequently Japan had been used as a kind of base camp for allied forces fighting in the Korean War.

There were Americans, and to a lesser degree British, servicemen everywhere. The top jobs in the major companies, like banks, the oil industry, shipping, were held by Americans and Europeans. Public signs were generally in both Japanese and English, though the latter were occasionally somewhat inventive, such as a road sign on a roundabout, 'All Traffic Please Keep', and the advertisement for a private detective, 'Very Secret Agents Ltd'.

We found that 1950s Japanese had very great charm but also retained some of the arrogance with which they had been associated before and during the war. On the one hand, we found them helpful, hospitable, generous and sensitive. We made many friends, but at a slightly superficial level because there was such an enormous cultural gulf, such a difference of experience and of expectation. We admired their sense of beauty and tried to learn from it. However, even here they were starting from concepts strange to us. In *ikebana*, for example, their famous art of flower arranging, they were working to ideas that seemed to us to be almost coldly geometric, whilst to them these carefully structured arrangements have great spiritual significance.

Indeed, a deep spirituality was widely evident, particularly in their religious observance, whether in their traditional Shinto religion or as Christians. Many Japanese Christians saw no great paradox in retaining much of their Shinto practice in their household arrangements and even visited the temples - sometimes straight after church! Christ Church, Yokohama, had been the English Church before the war. By the time I became its Rector (alongside my Missions to Seamen work) it was at least sixty percent American and we used the services of the Episcopal Church rather than the Book of Common Prayer. I enjoyed my induction according to the American rite, with the church warden handing me the key to the church.

It was on the evening of my induction, as I knelt at the altar rail to prepare myself for the service, that I noticed for the first time something that must have been staring me in the face every time I had visited the church beforehand. The face of Christ on the crucifix was Japanese. That this discovery came as a shock to me says much about the narrowness of Western Christianity and began for me a new understanding of the universality of Christ.

In the war Christ Church had been used by the Japanese Anglican church, the *Nippon Seiko Kai*, and there was a priest, Stephen Iwai, who was in charge of that congregation. He lived in a house on site and the one next to it was occupied by the diocesan bishop, Isaac Nosse. Bishop Nosse was one of the few real saints I have met in my life and he humbled me by sharing his problems and, to some extent, his tasks because 'you've been trained in England, Father'! He did not count his own Kelham training as equivalent, for some reason. It was entirely typical of him that he insisted the house he occupied should revert to its original use as the Rectory and be immediately 'Westernised' for us whilst he moved elsewhere in the city. Our son Michael was born there and baptised by Bishop Nosse.

The contact between the two congregations was not always harmonious. This was in part due to the Japanese sensibilities after a lost war and the other factors to which I have already referred. They had 'owned' Christ Church in the war years and now found their old landlords returning and resented that they had to share 'their' place with us. The relationship was not helped by the fact that members of the American/British congregation were also still bearing the scars of war. Some of them were old Japan hands who had been interned and ill treated, or had come back and found their property stolen or misused. Others had lived through all the years of anti-Japanese feeling and were very ambivalent about their posting to this country. There was frequent disagreement over the extent of use of the church which the Western congregation would 'allow' the Japanese. Here too, there was a fundamental difference of cultures. On Sundays we had an 8am service, our main morning service a little later and the Sunday School would last little more than an hour. We would use other parts of the building for various social and training activities during the week. The

Japanese Christians arrived at, say, 11.a.m. on a Sunday and their service would spill over into related activities lasting non-stop till we arrived for Evensong and more or less had to drive them out. Americans are not used to queuing, least of all to get into Church!

Having said all that, it was good to work closely with the Japanese church. Bishop Nosse afforded me many opportunities and we still value a gift I received after conducting a retreat for his clergy. It was typical of the *Nippon Seiko Kai* of the period that they gave me a beautiful beaten gold picture of a Shinto temple for leading a Christian retreat!

My work with the Missions to Seamen brought me into contact with a very different type of Japanese and another facet of their character. Officialdom had suffered the greatest loss of face and consequently felt the most need to assert itself. In Post Office queues each customer still bowed deeply to the clerk and apologised for troubling the honourable servant of the government for a stamp! The hierarchy of who bowed how deeply to whom pervaded 1950s Japanese society.

For anything up to six days in succession the immigration police on the dock gates would wave a friendly greeting as I went through on my daily ship visits. Then they would stop me, as if they had never seen me before, demand to see my pass, look at it upside down and ask 'Which ship are you from?' When I remonstrated that they knew quite well I was not from a ship, they would ask, 'Are you passenger or crew?' Occasionally they arrested me because my papers, which had been issued by them, were allegedly not in order, but of course after keeping me at the police station for a few hours would inevitably release me, always brusquely with the suggestion that they were doing me an enormous favour. They were confused people who felt obliged to play out their own roles in what they perceived to be the tragedy of their country, but I must confess I feel considerably more tolerance of their position in long retrospect than I sometimes did at the time.

Women were at that time still treated in the old Oriental style. They were expected to wear traditional clothes and look beautiful, as indeed they did. They walked a few paces behind their husband or boy friend in public and knelt daintily by his side in the home after serving the food, to be fed the occasional morsel by him with his chop sticks. Other than that they were expected to live in the kitchen. We once observed the family life of an Australian acquaintance and his Japanese wife when we were invited to dine with them at their home in a small village near Kobe. He met us at the station and took us to his house where we were greeted by his wife. After the obligatory bowing she knelt at the door and proceeded to help her husband and myself to take off our shoes (but not Diane who, as a mere woman, had to take off her own). We next saw our hostess when she brought in the food, to be eaten seated of course on the tatami covered floor at a low table. She knelt dutifully by her husband throughout the meal occasionally to be fed titbits from his dish. She took no part in the conversation and moved only from her husband's side at the end of the meal - when it was time to clear away the dishes. We saw her only once more upon leaving the house when she submissively helped me back into my shoes, again leaving Diane to put on her own! In discussing his marriage, our Australian acquaintance insisted his Japanese wife would not want it any other way. To this day Diane and I fail to understand how he could have enjoyed a marriage so apparently lacking in any real companionship. However, there was quite clearly love and not just physical attraction in the relationship, as was evident in all the Japanese couples we knew.

One of the main employers in Yokohama at the time, and in the port of Kobe, where we also spent a time, was the sex industry. A British seafarer told me that the difference between prostitutes in Japan and elsewhere was that the Japanese girls showed affection and a kind of loyalty. On many occasions I witnessed 'working girls' waiting at the docks for the return of a ship whose crew members they had entertained on a previous visit. The reunions were always one-to-one as of separated lovers and of warmth very different from any similar situation in the West. These girls showed real pleasure at meeting again a young man with whom they had enjoyed, not only sex, but also obviously a kind of friendship, and the feeling on either side was not diminished by the fact that money changed hands. It was little wonder that we found it difficult to make the facilities at the Mission club and hostel seem attractive!

The emancipation and westernisation of Japan began very soon after our time there. When we revisited for a week on our way back from Peter's wedding in Australia in 1990, we found a very different place. Public signs and notices in English were a rarity, there were only a few European and American faces, the top jobs in industry and commerce were by and large no longer available to foreigners, and officials seemed a little more relaxed and courteous. Men and women were walking not just side by side, but arm in arm, and youngsters were 'snogging' just as openly as they do in England. When we were there in the 1950s we got a 1,000 yen for the pound sterling; now the pound was worth 225 yen. In our day people were earning only a few thousand yen per month. Now the famous Kobe beef cost about £65 a pound and people seemed able to buy it. No wonder the Japanese economy imploded. Naturally, the people looked much healthier than they did all those years ago, and the average height of the famously small Japanese has greatly increased.

John Berg, doing the same work for which I had gone there, very generously invited us to stay with him in his house on the site where ours had stood. Most specially, I was allowed to preach at Christ Church again after all that time. It was fascinating to see the job being done in a totally different climate. It was interesting that John, who had been there for very many years and arrived not all that long after we left, had a totally different perception of Japan and the Japanese and, of course, a much healthier one than that which we came away in 1957.

After our home leave in 1957, we were sent by the Missions to Seamen to Port Sudan where, as I have already mentioned, we stayed for only a very short time as we all suffered very badly from the incredible heat. Undoubtedly, for all the frustrations we sometimes encountered during our time in Japan, we both felt the Arab world of Northern Sudan in the 1950s strangely more difficult to relate to than that of the Japanese. One day I was invited to a garden party at which African chiefs from the South of the country were being entertained by the Arab prefect of the region. The southerners were insultingly patronised and the terrible events that have happened in the Sudan since and its very recent separation of North and South Sudan were clearly foreshadowed by the behaviour and attitudes I encountered that day.

We found Port Sudan, and even Khartoum, alien and somehow menacing, whereas in Japan we had found the very distinctive culture exciting and alluring.

# VIII

# IN EDUCATION

## Church Youth Work and Partnership

Just as I was beginning to feel that the time was right for me to move on from The Missions to Seamen and return to work more directly associated with education, I received a visit from Roy Herbert, Secretary of the youth council of the Church of England Board of Education. As a result of conversations with him and his colleagues, I was short-listed and interviewed to become the Bishop of Oxford's Youth Officer.

This was the time when youth service was really being put on the map nationally. The Albemarle Report set out a new vision and, in turn, led to the recognition of paid professionals and to the founding of the National College for the Training of Youth Leaders in Leicester. Then the Bessey Report addressed the training of voluntary leaders. This led to the establishment of local and national agencies through which such training would be organised in a partnership between the various voluntary organisations and the local education authorities.

If the parishes in the Oxford diocese expected me, as the first holder of my office, to focus on exclusive church youth organisations, they were to be disappointed. For three years I was privileged to work in close collaboration with the youth officers of the three Counties which make up the diocese – Oxfordshire, Buckinghamshire and Berkshire - and, at that time still, the City of Oxford and the County Borough of Reading. Together we agreed a relevant strategy for the provision of youth service

84

and the training of leaders and I believe that the church was able to make a significant contribution to the partnership. We were also the recipients of much valuable grant aid and I remain grateful for the close and surviving friendships forged with my LEA opposite numbers and with some of the officers of other voluntary organisations.

The job involved me in running or assisting at many courses for leaders and for young people. It brought me into contact with schools and the provision of school-based youth workers. Dr. Julia Dawkins was appointed health education adviser by the City of Oxford and she and I worked together on sex education programmes for schools and youth clubs. There was a famous occasion when the Bishop of Oxford, Harry Carpenter, rang me and was told by Diane that I was 'out, doing sex with Julia Dawkins'. We never found out what the somewhat otherworldly Bishop thought she meant.

Both professionally and personally, one of the most important things of the time in Oxford was that it brought about a close relationship with Culham College and its then new principal, John Barnett. I was later invited to become a Governor of the college and moderator of its youth tutors course.

Of course there were specifically Church aspects of the work. I visited every deanery synod, before they were called synods, most clergy chapters and a very large number of parishes and I set up a network of deanery youth chaplains. After about a year the dioceses appointed two assistant youth officers, who became the vicars of small parishes alongside their youth work. The highlights were two diocesan youth festivals, at which church and non-church youth organisations displayed their skills and interests in a great open air festival setting. At least one pop music band, which was to receive national fame and its place in the charts, made its debut at one of our festivals. Both festivals were opened by well known broadcasters of the period – the first by my school friend Richard Baker, and the second by Judith Chalmers. We ended with great thanksgiving services. 'Modern' church music was very much in vogue and the young people took many a new hymn or tune back home with them. In 1965 we took a party of young people from some 20 parishes to Lugano in Switzerland for an unforgettable week of sun, the Lake, worship and study, and lasting friendships. As we saw them off from Lugano station in the care of the two assistant youth officers, they determined to embarrass me by all leaning out of the train and singing 'Rule Britannia' at the top of their voices.

For me, the Oxford appointment was an opportunity to put into practice some of what I believed about the church being a servant of the community, rather than an inward looking and exclusive club. At the end of 1963 I published a Report, 'Fifteen Months', describing our experiment in partnership. I was subsequently invited to apply at a national level what I had tried to do in Oxford and in 1965 I moved to Westminster, to become leadership training officer at the Church of England Board of Education's youth council.

For the family this meant that we moved back into the parish of the Ascension in Wembley Park, where we had lived during the time at Missions to Seamen head office and where we had made many friends. Both incumbents there, first Bill Beveridge and then Peter Ball, generously gave me hospitality at their altar and in their pulpit.

## At the Centre

It was a good time in the Board of Education's history. Dr Kathleen Bliss was an inspiring and visionary general secretary. Harold Wilson (no, not the Prime Minister; the remarkable priest responsible for laity training and later to become Principal of Salisbury Theological College.) and Lawrence Reading in the Board's adult education council were introducing us all to an understanding of the dynamics which are at work in groups. In the youth council itself at least three of us in the team worked closely and happily together, having remained friends - John Waller, later to become Bishop of Stafford after parochial work in Rochester and St. Alban's diocese; David Manship, who went on to become diocesan director of education in the Winchester diocese and then Rector of Abingdon; and I.

We each had our own specific responsibilities - David for training of young people, John the clergy, and I youth leaders - and we all approached our work with slightly different emphases. What we had in common however, was a belief in the church's mission to those who do not necessarily fill pews, and a commitment to the kind of non-directive leadership of young people that enables rather than dictates. In all departments of the Board of Education we were trying to comprehend more fully how groups work. The training we offered addressed an understanding of roles and functions and how the life and effectiveness of a group can be maintained, rather than what to do in the church youth club on a Thursday night.

## Germans and Group Work

At one point David Manship and I went on a fact-finding trip to Germany. It revealed how very insecure the Germans felt even twenty years after the end of the war and that they were paranoid about not being considered 'democratic'. We saw the principal of a Training College addressing his students from a podium in a tiered lecture theatre and proclaiming in the most Germanic manner that 'We must be democratic!' Everyone we met, in church and state youth work alike, desperately wanted to hear about group dynamics and our non-directive approaches which were totally alien to them.

Shortly after that visit, I was invited to introduce some group dynamics seminars in Berlin, and subsequently elsewhere in Germany. I continued to do this for several years, even after leaving the staff of the Board, towards the end only supervising the group of German trainers I had trained and who had worked with me. I think I was one of the few people with knowledge in that field who also happened to be bi-lingual. Dr. Josephine Klein, then at Sussex University, with whom I had done a number of joint courses in this country, was another German speaker whom they later involved.

This close working relationship with a group of Germans was emotionally not easy for me. One cannot work in the area of group dynamics without breaking down between people the kind of barriers that form such a basic part of German social mores. Even today they address each other formally when we would long since have been on first name terms. I had to try and establish informality and personal closeness among my nucleus group of

Germans, whilst finding it hard not to speculate which of them had been Nazis. Further, in Berlin I had to be the slightly detached foreigner in what was in fact the city of my birth and childhood with many very personal memories. It was emotionally not an easy assignment.

One weekend I met with that little group of trainers in a little town near Hanover. On the Sunday afternoon I suggested we had a break and went on an outing together. In three cars I led them to the nearby village of Bergen Belsen, the location of the notorious Nazi concentration camp. As we looked round that expanse of awfulness – with its mass graves and memorial tablets, each marking thousands, even hundreds of thousand bodies - I was relieved to see one of my group, whom I knew to have been a Nazi, sobbing bitterly. On the other hand I was appalled that a young left-wing Lutheran pastor in the group not only seemed unmoved, but was able to express the view that 'it's not really much worse than Vietnam'. That outing did more to strengthen the life of the group than any amount of training had done. We all became much closer. I have retained a close friendship with the organiser of this venture, Hermann Oberländer and Diane and I have spent pleasant times with him and his wife on subsequent visits to Berlin. To this day we meet on Skype almost monthly.

The emphasis at the Youth Council was very much on partnership with statutory and other voluntary agencies, as it had been in my work in the Oxford dioceses. In that context it made sense that for a period in 1966 I was seconded to work with HMI on a series of courses for full-time youth officers and organisers at the National College in Leicester. The founding principal of the college, Ted Sidebottom, a senior HMI, was seconded to lead the courses, which he did with great sureness of touch and a commitment to learning in and from groups, whilst his successor as Principal, Peter Duke, provided splendid organisational support. I believe the courses contributed significantly to the quality of leadership and management in local authority and voluntary youth work. To be involved on the staff of these courses was a great privilege.

**The Church and Schools**

The time in Westminster was stimulating and brought me into contact with many interesting people. However, I had by now been in different kinds of itinerant ministry for ten years and felt that, in the words since made famous by ministers who wanted to see less of Mrs. Thatcher, I 'wanted to spend more time with my family'. Diane was spending far too many long periods on her own with the two boys and they must have sometimes wondered where their dad had got to. I was also beginning to find it frustrating to leave every situation just as it was beginning to get interesting or it was being challenged locally. I needed an on-going community in which I would have to take responsibility for the effectiveness of the ideas I had been commending to others.

Community, for me, meant school. I was thinking in terms of another teaching post or a chaplaincy if such a thing could be found in other than the independent sector. To my surprise, Kathleen Bliss suggested I should apply for the headship of Archbishop Temple's School in Lambeth. To my even greater surprise I got the job.

Temple's, virtually in the grounds of Lambeth Palace, had been a Church of England boys' Central School - a strange invention designed between the wars to bridge the gulf between Elementary, later Secondary Modern, Schools and the Grammar Schools. By the time I was appointed in 1967, this particular Central School had been amalgamated with two other church schools in the area and had become a mixed comprehensive. As was not unusual in those days of secondary reorganisation, some of Temple's senior staff had been dragged into the new situation kicking and screaming!

They did not like the new set-up and now they did not like this new Head, with his fancy ideas, like 'helping young people to learn rather than teaching them'. They certainly did not approve of a Head who would not tolerate corporal punishment. They did not understand the 'new' talk of curriculum development, pastoral organisation, shared decision making. They were even deeply unhappy about my reluctance to wear a teaching gown. Finally, their attitude to pupil admissions was inimical to the comprehensive principle and to partnership with our neighbouring schools.

For my part, I felt that I had not disguised my views in interview and that the Governors had appointed me to do what I had told them I would want to do. In the ensuing struggle I had total support from some of the staff and from three men outside the school to whom I shall always be grateful. Oliver Fiennes, Rector of Lambeth and chair of Governors, lived next to the school and backed me through thick and thin, unlike his lay successor in the chair, who was a constant obstacle in all we tried to achieve.

Mervyn Stockwood, as the diocesan Bishop of Southwark, took a close interest in what I wanted to do and supported both my programme and me personally with that warmth and enthusiasm of which he was famously capable. I belong to that large group of people who were enormously fond of Mervyn, warts and all, and owe him much.

The Archbishop of Canterbury, Michael Ramsey, was the school's Patron and could be expected to feel that it was sufficient he should lend his name in that way. He chose to do far more. He visited several times and presided at a major function. On such occasions, for all his strange shyness, he tried to get to know both staff and students. Even more remarkably, he found time to insist that I went to see him regularly to report on what I was doing. He would sit there, looking as though he were miles away, making the occasional affirmative noise, and one went away feeling he had not heard a word. Then at the next visit he would repeat, word for word, what I had said last time and ask about it. Indirectly too, through his staff officer, Robert Beloe, who was a school governor, Michael Ramsey actively supported me in my aims.

At the school we established a very close relationship with the local education authority (ILEA) and worked to their formula to assure a truly balanced comprehensive intake. Coincidently, the authority's district inspector was a fellow Old Boy of Kilburn Grammar, a near contemporary with whom I had many mutual friends. The experience at Temple's confirmed my view that church schools should serve those who most need the love and care which we affirm, and there were many in Lambeth with that need. The church primary schools, locally and more widely in the diocese, protested that we did not always give preference to their brightest and best from well supported church homes. I understood their problem and tried to retain amicable working relationships with them. Yet I simply could not and still cannot, share their priorities.

I believe the church expends resources of money, plant and manpower on maintaining church secondary schools, resources that could be better used in the training of teachers, who could take the Christian ethos into non-church schools. To this day we have so-called comprehensive church schools that do everything in their power to be as un-comprehensive as they can. They claim the right to admit first, and without regard to any agreed catchment areas, those young people whose families claim to attend church. Thus they create islands of middleclass respectability in areas in which the other schools are left to cater for a disproportionate number of the deprived, the social misfits and the least able. Those church schools are not the kind of schools in which I would want to work, and they do not represent a doctrine of the church to which I can subscribe.

At Archbishop Temple's School (later amalgamated with St. Michael's School, Camberwell, and renamed Archbishop Michael Ramsey School) not only some staff, but even the older students did not like the kind of openness and re-thinking which I tried to introduce. The P.T.A. too, consisted to a large extent of parents who regretted that we were not still a single sex Central School and who feared I might destroy the school's image of being the 'respectable' school in a rough neighbourhood.

It was enjoyable at last to be in the Southwark diocese; to have the chance to get to know John Robinson and many others whose names one associates with the great theological Renaissance of the 1960s. However, at Archbishop Temple's my time was neither totally happy nor particularly successful. I achieved only a little of what I set out to do, though it could be said that I 'disturbed the peace' of the place and that it was never the same again after I had upset it. However, after just under four years I felt I could win the odd battle but not the war, and I decided I had to move on and that I wanted to work in a non-church school. I was, of course, grateful for the opportunity I had been given to learn some of the practicalities of headship and to develop my ideas in a school community.

Should I have been more successful at Archbishop Temple's School? Certainly I lacked experience of headship and had been out of touch with some of the administrative minutiae of running a school. Yet my administration of the place was commended even by some who did not share my ideals. The problem was, I believe, rather more fundamental. I was, and remained, committed to principles of shared leadership. I sought an approach to education in which the adults would have to learn to relate in a way in which they should then relate to their pupils, and in which they would encourage the young people to relate to each other. That philosophy is incompatible with a Head autocratically imposing change. There were those at the school who would have responded to directive leadership. I did not believe that this would be either an effective or an honest route to the ends I desired. I have never claimed that the way in which I believe a school should be run is the only way, or indeed, the only right way. However, once appointed to head a school after making no secret of these ideas, the method becomes non-negotiable.

Further, the problem about church secondary schools raises for me fundamental questions of politics and morality. I question the right of a religious organisation to demand the money of taxpayers who do not share the religious convictions, in order to build, maintain, staff and equip its schools, without attempting to ensure the benefit of such schools to the taxpaying community at large. As long as, in so many places, church secondary schools exist almost exclusively for the benefit of 'our own people', they should depend on the sacrificial giving of those they set out to serve. It can be convincingly argued that, in the primary sector, church schools historically play quite a different, more community-centred, role. I cannot be persuaded that these arguments are convincing in the secondary sector and I dislike the enthusiasm of politicians of both parties in the recent past for 'faith schools'.

My objections to church secondary schools apply as strongly to any other exclusive and divisive form of education. It is intolerable that, by tax concessions and in other ways, the state should enable private schools to cream off students and weaken the effectiveness of the comprehensive system. I find it totally unconvincing when people talk of their right to buy private education for their children if they can afford it. It creates social elites and social ghettos and, if it cannot be stopped, it should at least not be encouraged by society at large through fiscal and structural support. It is only because of financial benefits, which should be shared more widely, that such schools sometimes seem able to do things better than those in the public sector. They are not in themselves better schools and socially their existence does as much disservice to those who attend them as those who cannot. Needless to say I find the current deliberate vandalism of the local education authorities by the creation of hundreds of academy schools and, more recently still, the ridiculous 'free schools' totally repulsive.

**The Big Challenge**

On the strength of the headship experience in Lambeth I began to apply for similar posts in larger schools. I was short-listed each time and was twice told that I was a 'close runner up' at the interviews. I would have been offered the headship of a school in a Lancashire industrial town, however Diane came with me for the two days of interviews and we both felt we simply could not live there. Two weeks later I went for an interview at Don Valley High School in Doncaster. This large and quite well known school was the one I was sure I could not hope to get, and by lunchtime on the first day I was offered it. I suppose it could be argued that I was only appointed because the interviewing procedures were so inadequate and rushed!

Don Valley had been a Grammar School and was amalgamated shortly before I went there with a Secondary Modern School, which had only a year previously been moved into a new building on the same site. There was some separatism between the two buildings, which were now being used as lower and upper schools, and some staff thought it a great hardship to move between two buildings on one campus. I just found it a great relief to be away from the problems of three widely separated sites on which we operated at Archbishops Temple's.

It was a great relief in many other ways, too. The school was well provided by way of buildings and equipment, with on-site playing fields and even our own indoor swimming pool. A majority of the staff was willing to listen and think together about what we were doing and why we were doing it. Most important of all, the senior management team - consisting at that stage of a Deputy Head, a Senior Mistress (of Deputy Head status but with a title which was a hangover from Grammar School terminology), and Heads of Upper and Lower School - accepted that I had ideas and ideals which might be new to them but were willing to work as a team with me. A year later Jeff Jakes, the Deputy Head whom I had found in post, left to take up a headship. I was most grateful for the very generous support he gave me as a newcomer and I knew I would miss him, but the appointment of a successor marked a necessary break with the previous regime. A Second Deputy joined us soon afterwards and there was a change of head of Upper School. When I pressed for the appointment to that post of the only woman on the shortlist, the governors needed a good deal of persuading that 'a lass can keep them in order!' Eileen Shaw, who joined us from Holland Park School in London, did keep them in order and did much more than that.

In Lambeth, for all the problems, I had the support of an excellent local education authority (ILEA). I was equally fortunate now to be working in the West Riding, under the inspiring leadership of Sir Alex Clegg and with his two deputies. The ill-judged 1974 Local Government Reorganisation ended the West Riding and brought us into the new Doncaster Metropolitan District. This was a small authority by comparison and correspondingly limited in vision and scope, although staffed generously and by well-intentioned and generally congenial officers.

It is easy to forget that in those days every school tended to have a clearly defined catchment area. It was before the days of free parental choice, which has resulted in the dreadful competitive marketing between neighbouring schools. Even a few years ago we would have found this utterly distasteful. Don Valley drew everyone from seven primary schools in 'village' suburbs of Doncaster, most with predominantly coal-mining populations. In terms of social class the intake resembled that at Archbishop Temple's, yet it was entirely different. I had not worked in the

97

North before and was enchanted, if also sometimes a little irritated, by that which is distinctively Yorkshire. I found the people blunt in a manner I liked greatly, and surprisingly welcoming to a 'foreigner' from London. I also found them chauvinist and discovered that to live in a one-party state - even when it is one's own party- has serious drawbacks. Too much business, whether of the Council or of bodies like school governors, was conducted in small cliques over the consumption of large quantities of beer in miners' and working men's clubs. I sometimes felt that some of the more important decisions at governors' meetings had been taken before the agenda was even published. Sadly, these tendencies seem to have run amok in recent years and the saga of the 'Donny-gate scandal' has become only too well publicised. Some of the local people I worked with during my time there were difficult, sometimes boorish, but they were not corrupt. A few were bigoted and bore scars of the social history of the area, but most were men of great enthusiasms and considerable integrity and when we differed I was never in doubt that they had the school's good at heart.

I met strange differences in parental attitudes from those to which I had been used in Lambeth. There, for example, the parents had pleaded with me to persuade their sons and daughters to stay on at school as long as possible. In Doncaster, many said, "Johnny has this silly idea that he wants to go into the Sixth Form. You'll tell him, won't you, that he ought to go and get a job". There was also a subtle difference between the discipline problems encountered by teachers in the two places. I found difficulties of class control which staff experienced in the North less easy to understand. I knew where I was with London boys and girls but at times had to have the Doncaster youngsters interpreted to me by my 'native' colleagues. Yet kids are kids and by and large those at Don Valley were among the most delightful I had ever met.

Within a year of my arrival, the Authority changed Don Valley from a 12-form to a 14-form entry. This meant we had 420 students in each school year and, additionally, a Sixth Form. We had to develop new strategies for pastoral care to assure that no one was lost in such a large crowd. Indeed, structures of communication on every level became my chief concern. I have written much more fully elsewhere about my educational philosophy and the structures it involves. What I believe about the running of a comprehensive school is best summed up as *'From the Head Upwards'*, and my book by that name was published in 2001. I tried at Don Valley to introduce an inverted pyramid. In it the Head is at the foot, holding things up, with other members of senior management above him. Then come middle managers of the academic and pastoral structure. Right at the top, which in the traditional hierarchy would be the base line, we place those at the chalk face – the subject teachers and form tutors. Clearly, the students are then in a line above that. They are the ones that ultimately benefit from the strength of this supportive structure.

To implement such a philosophy, it was necessary to put in place a staff council of middle managers (heads of departments and of year groups) at which colleagues were weaned from the traditional battle, each for their own empire, to a collaborative consideration of whole-school matters. The very existence of the council also helped to overcome the dichotomy between pastoral and academic, which can be so detrimental to the health of schools.

Staff meetings, departmental and year group meetings, the daily bulletin, staff briefings, all had to take on shapes that would undergird the supportive and decision-sharing philosophy. The students, too, had to be involved in this strategy, so form, year and school councils were formed and eventually encouraged to work with minimal staff input.

The underlying principle was that everyone had to be empowered to do their particular job as teachers or learners. Everyone had to be convinced that they wanted to be what would now be called stakeholders in our corporate enterprise. This had far-reaching consequences in the way we had to communicate with each other and the methodologies we adopted. I was not offering my colleagues on the staff easy options and the response of a majority of them was exceedingly generous. Some were, as would be expected, so entrenched in the ways to which they had been previously exposed, that they were resistant to, and suspicious of, our motives. It was hurtful to be accused by a senior head of department of 'deviousness' when I invited him to share more in the decision- making process.

Any progress we were able to make depended on the strength and commitment of the senior management team. The success of the school in terms of this philosophy was in direct proportion to the successful working of the team. We were a very disparate group. Some had been at the school for many years whilst others of us were "incomers". One of the team had come from a school where innovation had been the accepted order. Some were so steeped in the traditions of their previous years in education that what I was doing came as a considerable shock; nor were they easily convinced. Mostly the group was willing, however, to challenge the old ways, hoping that a different approach would be more successful. All of them - Alan Brookman, Brian Oglethorpe, Marian Holman, Eileen Shaw and Colin Burley – were far more loyal than I had any right to expect. Together we took corporate responsibility for what went wrong, when they could have so easily blamed me and my 'new notions'. We grew closer because we were prepared to invest time in our being together and allow ourselves the space to talk of more than just everyday practicalities. So most of us began to appreciate our diversity of talents and our interdependence. We became, and have remained, friends.

All schools, but especially such large ones, are delicate mechanisms that need constant fine-tuning. They require sensitive leadership, which I aimed to give but probably never really mastered. Nevertheless, I believe we achieved more than we would have done with a more conventional approach.

Without doubt, the headship of Don Valley High School was the big challenge of my life. Not a day passed without my being grateful that I had been given this opportunity, or without being overawed by its enormity. I loved the place and the people. It is my great sorrow that my health was not good during this time, which finally forced me to leave sooner than I would have wanted.

**A secular ministry**

What then of my priestly ministry during those years in a 'secular' working environment. I had been invited to meet the staff a few weeks before taking up the post, and on that occasion a number of questions clearly showed that my being ordained posed a threat to some of them. 'What shall we call you?' they asked, and I suggested, 'Try "Your Eminence"'. I took soundings and decided, at least initially, to drop the 'Rev.' on the school notepaper.

Soon after my arrival I was visited at school by a succession of local clergy, who were naturally curious. I found myself saying, 'Have you come to ask whether I'm here because I have lost my faith, or are you asking whether I am available to take occasional services?' The answer to both questions, I told them, was no. In fact, I did not find this aspect of my new situation very amusing. Although I had done mainly non-parochial jobs, my view of my ministry was a fairly sacerdotal ('priestly') one. I had always had the hospitality of someone's altar and pulpit and I was going to feel deprived without regular opportunities to celebrate Communion and to preach. I would feel denuded without my dog collar.

Two factors helped me. Primarily, I knew that my work at the school was going to be totally demanding, for long hours every day and on seven days a week. It would have been impractical to have committed myself to other duties. In no way could I be called a Non Stipendiary Minister. At the same time, the more I missed the ecclesiastical part of my ministry, the more I was also becoming angry, or at least disappointed, that the church's hierarchy seemed so disinterested in my spiritual welfare, that it failed, in fact, to acknowledge my existence. No local priest invited me to keep in touch, once I had said I could not offer to help, no Rural Dean or Archdeacon visited or enquired, no invitation was issued to any kind of function or organisation. In retrospect, I acknowledge that this was, in part, my own fault and that I used it as an alibi - but only in part. I was surprised a priest could be thought fit by secular authority to do such a big job in education, but his church didn't seem to consider it was involved.

I did not feel that I had in any sense left the church or abandoned my ordained ministry. I was totally immersed in the job I was doing and incredibly busy. I did not seriously question that what I was doing was in fulfilment of my priestly vocation, but I must confess that during those years I had periods of real doubt about the church in which I am priest. I was, I suppose, in a term later applied in politics, 'semi detached'.

# IX

# THE SWINGING SIXTIES... AND THE SWING BACK

## A much maligned decade

Anyone the greater part of whose life was in the 20th century will probably mark out the war period of the 1940s as the most historically significant. Other decades will be placed into some order of importance, depending on personal experience and awareness. Few however, can fail to have been aware of the meaningfulness of the Sixties.

According to the warm beer and village cricket brigade - of both political parties and both genders - a group of malevolent conspirators set out in about 1961 to subvert civilisation. Evil people, usually 'pinkos' or 'loony lefties', destroyed all that is held most dear – the family, the church, the arts, the media - and, of course, warm beer! These same destroyers of 'traditional values' then went on to invent sex, which is apparently the root of all evil.

It is claimed, on the one hand, that the perpetrators of this plot against society were intellectual and cultural pygmies; on the other hand, it is suggested that the plot was so fiendishly clever that it succeeded completely and did untold damage to the social fabric.

As none of the critics are particularly young, one wonders where they were in the Sixties. They did not, on the whole, (*pace* Mary Whitehouse) make much noise at the time. Nor does the experience of most of us who lived through that decade bear any resemblance to the recollection or ex post facto assessment of these self-appointed guardians of tradition. (Conversely it is sometimes said, half seriously, that those who really lived in the Sixties would have been in no state to remember them!)

As I look back on my life, it is inevitable that I should make special mention of this significant decade. Unfortunately one can only touch on some of the important things that happened during that time and I have neither the space, nor indeed the qualifications, to offer more than a brief critique and, probably, a rather subjective one.

Certainly the period from, say, 1962 to about 1975 was one of the most exciting through which I have lived. The events of the decade are in retrospect inevitably telescoped. It did not all occur at once, nor everywhere simultaneously, and it took several years before some new ideas and practices overtaking London affected other parts of the country.

## A great Renaissance

The really significant thing about the Sixties is its spontaneous combustion. People had grown up in the pretty dismal Thirties, suffered quite dreadfully in war, and then endured the austerity of the following decade. The Fifties really were grim, with seemingly never-ending rationing of food and clothing, shortages, and terrible drabness, of which 'utility furniture' was just one dire example. There was a sickly glamorisation of war in films and books. Only a very few enjoyed the kind of 'luxuries' which very many more people now take for granted, and the height of holiday expectation for thousands was a wet and draughty week of hearty regimentation in a Butlin's chalet at Skegness or Pwllheli.

In a way the transition from all that to something a bit better was modestly initiated by a new kind of music from the likes of Cliff Richard and Adam Faith. After that, things started to change dramatically. For many there are two quite disparate key events that mark out their awareness of the period; the bursting of the Beatles onto the scene, and the *Lady Chatterley's Lover* obscenity trial.

Of course, there was much more. In music the Beatles were not alone; the pop phenomenon existed not just in its own right, but reflected the mood of the period and it was matched by innovative 'serious' music. In 1962 Diane and I met two of the Beatles at one of my uncle's showbiz parties. In retrospect it is incredible that they were as yet so little known that we cannot now remember which of the 'Fab Four' we met that night. By the end of the year they were household names.

In Art new and stimulating work was being done. In literature a new generation of authors attracted a whole new generation of readers. Exciting cinema and theatre flourished. In fashion even men cared about what they wore and flocked to the new boutiques in Carnaby Street

The important common factor in all areas of Sixties Renaissance was its spontaneity and how innovation in one sphere mirrored the aspirations and experiments in every other. Certainly there were outstanding prophets of newness; but they reflected what people themselves were already beginning to think and want; those who led were responding to the silent aspirations and instincts of thousands. There was a great awakening, a re-birth of liveliness and excitement, not least in three key areas – politics, theology and the ethics of personal relationships.

## The years of Revolutions

Much of the rest of this chapter may appear more a history lesson than an autobiography. However, the events of that period, my reflections on them, and the political conclusions that I draw are very much 'me'. Had I not lived through that remarkable decade I would be a different person and I therefore cannot apologise for dwelling on these happenings as I have done.

Most of us were taught at school that in the $19^{th}$ century 1848 was The Year of Revolutions throughout Europe. One hundred and twenty years later the world had shrunk and a new spirit of revolt was felt not only in Europe, but also in the Americas, in the Far East and in the emerging nations of Africa and Asia.

We forget too easily that this period, which we associate with changes in our own society, was that in which the map of the formerly colonised continents was redrawn. The subsequent history of some of the nations that began to find their freedom and identity at this time is not a totally happy one. It does not alter the fact that they did achieve their independence in a universal climate of change and that millions in the West, who had been apathetic to events in distant lands, acquired a new world-awareness. This, in turn, gave rise to the anti-apartheid movements, the boycotts of South African goods, the concern of many about racial discrimination and other injustices in the United States. In their struggle for dignity in their own nations, Martin Luther King and Nelson Mandela engaged the spirit of people everywhere.

In the Western world, the brutal war the Americans fought in Vietnam was one of the catalysts. In Washington they burnt their draft cards; in London we converged on the American embassy in Grosvenor Square, and they demonstrated in Paris, Amsterdam, Berlin and even in Sydney. There was a sense of outrage at the obvious wrongness of what was happening, especially as more became known of the conduct of some American servicemen in Vietnam. Young people everywhere - and many who were not so young - were outraged by the deviousness and hypocrisy of politicians in the USA and in the countries supporting the war. The hopes reflected by Harold Wilson's successive election victories in 1964 and 1966 were dampened by his unwillingness to condemn outright the Americans in that despicable enterprise. The assassination of President Kennedy in 1963 had brought the Camelot dream of many young people to a premature end. By 1967 and 1968, shocked as people were by the murder of President Kennedy's younger brother and likely successor, Robert Kennedy, they were beginning to see the Kennedy image as slightly tarnished and this added to the sense of political frustration. The violent death of Martin Luther King was one further tragic setback.

The anti-Vietnam War protest was, however, also symptomatic of a wider sense of grievance in many countries against established authority that had held sway unchallenged for far too long. The 1968 student demonstrations, particularly in Paris, were expected by many to be the beginning of a great international uprising. Of course it didn't happen. Not for the first time in the history of revolutions, when the intellectuals tried to involve the proletariat, the workers felt strongly but were less energetic and had reason to be more afraid of possible repercussions. Also, again not for the first time, if the students and workers in the United Kingdom had matched the enthusiasm of their Continental counterparts, it would have made a difference; we learned again that revolution and the British way of life do not seem to go together.

In Jeremy Paxman's recent book 'The English', George Steiner is quoted as saying, '...this land is blest by a powerful mediocrity of mind. It has saved you from communism and it has saved you from fascism. In the end you don't care enough about ideas to suffer their consequences.' Sometimes one shares this perception with a sense of frustration. Yet, there are probably more times when we have cause to be very thankful for this, as for so many other characteristics of Britishness or, perhaps, more accurately, Englishness.

However, the spirit of revolution was pervasive. Even at Archbishop Temple's school, with its tradition of conformity, the student body twice in 1968 staged walk-outs to the neighbouring park in protest against some edict that they thought had come from me. My colleagues were outraged at the action. I approved the action but disapproved the cause. The young people of course just saw the disapproval but not the distinction I was making.

It is easy now to dismiss the political events of the Sixties as damp squibs. They were not, because things have never been the same again. One thinks back to the diffidence with which Richard Dimbleby ushered senior politicians into the Panorama studio for hitherto unheard of public exposure, yet treating them with so much obsequiousness that the message rarely got across. Within a very short time we had moved from that climate to the satirical *That Was The Week That Was* and iconoclastic stage revues like *Beyond the Fringe.* The politicians helped by revealing themselves to be utterly ridiculous, as in the Tory collapse over the Profumo affair and the absurd succession as Prime Minister to Harold Macmillan of Lord (Alec Douglas) Home, a veritable caricature of political naive, but arrogantly, landed gentry. In common with the Cholmondleys and the Featherstonehaughs the man did not even pronounce his name as it was written!

Not surprisingly, then, weak politicians in later years regret that in the Sixties the public suddenly ceased to give blind respect to people simply by virtue of the office they hold. It is not this that has subverted the fabric of society, nor has the fact that television can shine bright light on previously secret corners of political drawing-rooms. Unfortunately, as part of Thatcher philosophy and its inheritance, rather too many politicians have shown an arrogance and self-indulgence which ignored that in the modern world they were bound to get found out. They, the very people who would blame everything on the Sixties, have done untold harm to the perception of politics by ordinary people. Healthy democracy requires that all should feel involved and should wish to participate. This is sadly no longer the case.

Politically the Sixties were stimulating and those of us on the left had reason to hope that the world was moving in our direction. Much of what was going on in the USSR was depressing and, just when we thought the communist leaders had learned from the error of their Hungarian adventure in 1956, they repeated it all in Czechoslovakia. Not everything on that side of the 'iron curtain' was, however, as bad as leaders in the West would claim; I enjoyed and learned from visits to the (Communist, East) German

Democratic Republic. Its regime was oppressive, its secret police unacceptable, yet today in the reunified Germany many in the East are nostalgic for some of what they remember of that time. Further, the more we learn of the excesses of, for example, the CIA and MI6, Mossad and other Western intelligence agencies, the more we have to ask who should cast the first stone.

**Theology and Behaviour**

For some of us, probably the most exciting aspect of the Sixties was the emergence of new thinking in theology during those years.

There is one name above all others among the contributors to this revolution in thought and that is, of course, John Robinson, then Bishop of Woolwich. It is significant that when his *Honest to God* was published in 1963 he was more surprised than most by the furore it produced. I can understand this. As I read the book my reaction was, 'This is what I've been thinking and saying. How wonderful that it has now been so brilliantly laid out.'

Not only had my own thinking been so similar, *Honest to God* expressed what I had been hearing from intelligent Christians of all age groups. In his Preface to the book, John Robinson says, '... as I watch or listen to a discussion between a Christian and a humanist, I catch myself realising that most of my sympathies are on the humanist's side.' This reflected the experience of many of us, not because we had lost our faith in God, but because we shared Robinson's anxiety to express these things anew for ourselves and for the many thousands who had not any longer been hearing us at all.

We recognised a Christian humanism, even a Christian agnosticism, which we knew would be hurtful to those steeped in unquestioning acceptance of traditional doctrine. None of us, I sincerely believe, failed to respect those Christians who did not share what we were thinking and saying, although we were sad, and sometimes angry, that they so often did not seem to reciprocate our respect.

We shall never know just how many people were helped by *Honest to God*, and the other books by John Robinson published within a short time afterward in popular editions. In the church the books gave entitlement to those who had previously wanted to say very similar things and perhaps had not dared, and to a new spirit of open discussion. Beyond the clergy and their congregations large numbers of thoughtful men and women were prepared to enter into dialogue with a church they had for some time been finding intellectually unattractive, or simply boring.

The writings of the period did not significantly change the pattern of church attendance, except perhaps to make some Christians wonder whether they had neglected other important aspects of their religion by involvement solely in worship. There were not, as far as I know, many 'converts'. The prime effect was that the church was, slowly, again being accepted as a partner in the great debate about the nature of the world in which we live, the purpose of life and the way in which we should relate to each other. This change came about not so much as a result of what John Robinson and others were saying to secular society. Rather, by saying what they did to thinking Christians, they empowered us to enter into conversations in which others would want to hear us and be able to understand us. I consider myself very fortunate to have had the privilege of knowing John Robinson and learning from his mouth and not only his pen. I owe much to the support he gave me at that time and, of course, to the intellectual stimulation.

The new theology needed to be interpreted in terms of human behaviour and no one did more towards that than my friend Douglas Rhymes. Outstandingly in *No New Morality,* he questioned whether the traditional moral code of authoritarianism and an unvarying law really was the teaching of Christ, or rather a perversion of it. He and others helped to point the way to a morality which was not new, but which had been lost - the morality of love, of basing our conduct towards one another on the integrity of the individual. He went on shortly afterwards to set out a clear spiritual dimension to his previous work in *Prayer in the Secular City,* picking up in the title the work of the earlier *The Secular City,* by the American Harvey Cox. Douglas was viciously and very personally attacked by those who can only see ethics in terms of sex.

There is no space to name all the others who contributed to the great outflowing of exciting new theological thinking. Many of them were influenced to some extent by the life and work of Dietrich Bonhöffer and Reinhold Niebuhr.

## A Responsible Society

During the Sixties I was heavily involved in leading courses for young people and their leaders. There was a tendency for all courses, whatever their published purpose, to home in very quickly on questions of relationships. This was due largely to the fact that training tended at that time to be non-directive and that we set out to address people where they were, rather than where we might want them to be. Clearly they were at the point of needing to think out their views on human inter-relationships.

If we wanted to help teachers and youth leaders to think more deeply about their work, rather than give them successful lesson material or simple recipes for youth club programmes, it was natural that they should want to address how they related with one another in their own teams, their relationships with their young people, and their attitudes towards the relationships among the young people. Similarly, the young themselves felt that everything of importance to them hinged on how they dealt with each other.

Almost everyone we met in these situations seemed instinctively to be reflecting what the pundits were calling situational ethics. To the traditionalists this was of course anathema. They believed then, as they had always done and still do, that there are inflexible rules which need to be applied to all situations and which provide safe and sure guidelines in all our human conduct. Moral philosophers and theologians, teachers and students, youth workers and their members, were all - more or less independently from each other - challenging this legalistic view.

The old ways had self-evidently not worked all that well. More importantly, the 'safe' rules had in fact meant that people need not stop to think about their behaviour at all. Better, it was now argued, that each new situation requires us to consider how best to behave in it with maximum benefit to all involved and with minimum hurt to anyone.

Of course it was sometimes simplistic and there was a danger of throwing out the baby with the bath water. In practice, however, far from always seeking new answers, people did ask each other, 'How did *you* tackle this when you had to?' In seeking their own solutions to their moral dilemmas, young people had a new and more urgent curiosity about the traditional teachings; but they demanded the right to re-examine their relevance. It would be naive to deny the dangers inherent in basing all morality on the 'do unto others...' precept or on the view that anything goes as long as it can be shown that 'no one gets hurt'. Nevertheless, it was a hallmark of the Sixties (and, for that matter, most of the Seventies) that people, and especially the young, were curiously concerned with moral decisions and their effect on others.

This was indeed a new morality, in the sense that many were thinking out their morals for the first time and were not prepared to follow traditional teaching with blind obedience. It is also important to remember that the traditional teachings had long been more honoured in the neglect than in the observance and that this generation of young people had inherited a pretty mucky world.

We all know that the rejection of some handed-down views and practices, not least in sexual relationships, was far reaching and led not only to new freedoms, new positive discoveries about oneself and others, but also to new areas of unhappiness for some. Not everything that happened was of as much benefit to those involved as they may have felt at the time. Yet, the enormous growth of tolerance, of acceptance of others' different way of life and solutions, has to be acclaimed as a great step forward.

Many were liberated by the availability of the contraceptive pill. Women experienced a new entitlement to sexual freedom and enjoyment and they, perhaps more even than men, discovered that it was not necessarily adultery, but rather dishonesty between partners, which was the true cause for relationships breaking down. Monogamy, which has never been as 'biblical' as the traditionalists claim, took a knock during this time. One of the positive spin-offs was a new understanding that people owed each other the respect of open and honest dealing and commitment appropriate to their relationship, but that they did not own each other.

Although even now, half a century later, there is still much homophobia and discrimination on the grounds of sexuality, the Sixties did see the scandalously delayed part-implementation of the *Wolfenden Report* and small but significant changes in the draconian laws against gay people. The greater sexual openness and awareness made many more tolerant, especially as they discovered elements of bi-sexuality in themselves, or at least that which the former Archbishop of York, Dr David Hope, has described as 'a grey area'.

**So what went wrong?**

It was clearly not enough. Too many were not touched by the great revolutions and discoveries. Too many others felt threatened by them. Further, progressive ideas tend to go with a favourable economic climate. Harold Wilson's 'white heat of technology', the founding of the Open University and the relative affluence of the Sixties became all too soon the devaluation of the pound and then the economic crises of the Seventies. Within a very few years we had Margaret Thatcher and the most devastating backlash.

We have, since the period of exciting new thought and behaviour, lived through the horrors of Thatcherism, with its overt denial of the very existence of society. We have seen the new awakening of altruism, of sensitive awareness of our neighbour, replaced by the gospel of greed, the glorification of the entrepreneur and the submission of everything to 'market forces'.

We then had a 'New' Labour government that did many good things. How sad, therefore, that it seems, unbelievably, to have espoused many similar ideas and to continue the Tory assault on those who should be its natural partners, such as teachers, doctors, nurses, social workers. Like the most right wing of Tories who are their successors, the 'New' Labour government, too, spoke of 'zero tolerance' and of 'condemning more than understanding'. Children who do not find it easy to conform are now criminalised. The unemployed, the sick and the socially incompetent are compelled to prove that they are not 'scroungers' and the welfare state - once Britain's proudest boast - is a 'safety net' for those who submit to a means test. Caring single parents are told that seeking a job is more important than providing a stable and loving home environment. Those who seek asylum are not welcome and, of course, prison, they say, 'works'.

I have referred in the previous chapter to the damage done to a once admirable education system. The comprehensive ideal has been ridiculed and replaced with academies, free schools, and the penalising of the most vulnerable by abolishing the Education Maintenance Grant and other supportive structures.

The petty nationalism and xenophobia of sections of the press has encouraged the emergence of some very frightening attitudes in a nation once renowned for its tolerance and its appreciation of the benefits of a multi-cultural society. I can only be grateful that I was a refugee here at a time when it was deemed a matter of pride to offer a welcome to the stranger, when the nation was sufficiently self-confident to feel unthreatened by the alien and the unknown.

It was, for my generation of socialists, deeply depressing that in 1995, after the untimely death of John Smith, our once democratic party was hijacked by people who shared none of our ideals. We are, of course, accused of being out of date and out of touch. That is to mistake philosophy for tactics. I can accept the accommodations with market economy which may be forced on a left of centre government in the capitalist world of today. I cannot accept that one should not wish it were otherwise and seek to infuse that system with socialist ideals and mechanisms. I cannot accept the abdication of principle for the pursuit of power. I reject the thesis that there is no difference between a democratic socialist and some wishy-washy liberal who has a sneaking regard for the underdog. I live with the hope that the present Labour Party leadership will use its hopefully short period in opposition to return us to our roots.

I deplore the view that businessmen always know best and that, therefore, they must be involved in partnership with, or instead of the public sector in education, health and everywhere else. This is expediency - a way of tapping 'private' funds rather than risking unpopularity by asking the community to pay for services by the old principle of 'from each according to their means'. Public services should be run by well trained professionals with appropriate philosophies, not by those who hold the purse strings, be they bureaucrats or entrepreneurs. It is totally unacceptable that public services on which we all depend, most especially health, education and the social services, should be provided by those in 'private enterprise, whose foremost aim must be to make a profit. The most recent revelations of the immorality of bankers and press barons ought to make us question the constant urge by politicians to hand the running of the country to 'the private sector'.

Perhaps the experience of the Sixties, the partial realisation of a better and more open society, makes the disappointments of the last thirty-plus years so particularly hard to bear. Those of us who lived through the much-maligned decade need no reminder that some of what happened then was far from perfect; but it was a great deal better than what has happened since.

# X

# CANCER

## That other country

In 1982 my voice started to do funny things. At first it was an almost imperceptible hoarseness but gradually my speaking sounded more and more strained, although I was not conscious of any great discomfort. I had reported a similar problem earlier and was told that my larynx was affected by an overall neurological condition on my left side, which was also producing other symptoms. Diane was, however, more concerned and asked our G.P. to examine my throat. She told him that there was what she described as, an 'illness smell'. When I next saw him he said, "Your wife tells me you need a mouth wash", but he did not look at my throat!

Eventually, early in 1983, things became intolerable. I had begun to cough and splutter quite badly and, after one particularly awful night, Diane told the doctor that I simply had to be referred to a specialist at once. He phoned back later in the day to say I had an appointment in a fortnight. "Nonsense", said Diane (whom people tend to think of as a meek and mild person!) "It has to be tomorrow". Her forcefulness, in the face of the only really bad G.P. we have ever encountered, almost certainly saved my life.
I should confess here that many years earlier, and against all my political convictions, I had enrolled, when my teachers' union offered favourable group membership, in a private health insurance plan. I am ashamed to say that I am very squeamish when it comes to other people's illnesses – a shockingly bad visitor of the sick - and I like privacy when I am not well. Of course, this health insurance contributed to the speed with which I was

120

seen, on the next day, and to the comfortable surroundings in which I subsequently found myself, although I know that I would have received the same care under the N.H.S. It is sadly true that it might, however, have been too late. Such inequality of life chances is of course deplorable.

The consultant, Mr. Keith Thomas, and I 'clicked' at once. He will be embarrassed that I say publicly how much I admired and liked him and how his personal qualities contributed enormously to my confidence in him and in all that was about to happen. Some, when they become consultants, seem to protect their personae in a great mantle of self-importance, holding their patients, almost as untouchables, at arm's length. They should emulate the warmth and humility of others among their colleagues, like Mr.Thomas. I do not mean he is hearty, which is another objectionable tendency of health professionals. He is quiet and gentle and totally uneffusive, but his personality conveys caring and integrity. I was so fortunate to be in his care.

To return to February '83. I expected Mr.Thomas to confirm that it was all due to a neurological weakness, but I had only said "Good Morning" when he responded, "I don't like the sound of that at all"! Within moments he had decided that he wanted to investigate a lump and insisted on an urgent biopsy. I found myself in the General Hospital the next day.

The recall, two days earlier than we had been told to expect, has to be described as traumatic. Mr. Thomas did not mince words. "If we do not do something about this very quickly, it will do something pretty final about you." Then came the detailed description of the malignancy and of the operation and how it would leave me. In the consultant's presence we were both remarkably calm and I even tried to make a rather sick joke about the whole thing. We wondered why a nurse followed us out of his room and seemed to tail us as we walked through the hospital. She was clearly not surprised that before we reached the exit we both broke down. Looking back after all these years, I remember our distress far less than our absolute determination that this was not going to kill me and that we would learn to live with a voiceless me.

I say 'we', and there is no doubt at all that it was Diane's courage and ability to share this, throughout that time and ever since, that enabled me to survive physically and emotionally. I cannot think what it must be like to face alone the situation that confronted me. We experienced together the sharing of fear as well as hope; the need to support each other whenever one of us was feeling particularly low; the discovery that 'in sickness and in health' was not just empty church rhetoric; the realisation that the one who is ill can contribute, however slightly, but always of course in lesser measure, to the one who isn't.

In the Three Shires Hospital, where I was admitted almost at once, I was prepared for the operation over two days, which allowed me to settle in, to meet those who would be dealing with me and to become more fully aware of what was to be done to me. In as much as this was a kind of counselling, it was helpful. I would plead that, before surgery with such dramatic outcomes, patients should be prepared a little more than I was, although I appreciate there was urgency. England has an absurdly large number of mutual 'support groups' for everything from cancer patients to those who suffer from ingrown toenails. Yet we seem to be sadly lacking in proper professional counselling before and after major surgery. There must be many like me, who are not particularly prone to navel-gazing, yet would welcome proper information about their condition from those whose job it is to know these things. Nor should it be left to the one busy surgeon who performs the actual operation.

After the operation I had the usual intensive care and was surrounded by all the paraphernalia of drips and transfusions as well as the specialist gadgetry required by this particular operation. I have to assume that my readers share my squeamishness and shall therefore not go into the gruesome details!

Predominantly, I remember the sense of deep shock when, on coming to, I found Diane and Michael by my bed and I said, "Well, we've won!" and then realised that, of course, I didn't say it. Despite the preparation, I had not really taken in that there just would not be a voice. No voice at all. I, who had spent a life of teaching, preaching, training, debating and being argumentative, had finally been reduced to complete silence.

One of the special things about cancer is that patients tend to have removed from them some vital part of their anatomy that they had, up to that point, taken for granted. They have to learn to live without something that had seemed indispensible. I began in hospital to think about the concept of cancer being 'another land'. Quite early on, I was watching the local news on television, when Diane came in. I asked her (in writing of course - all my communication in those days was on notepads) "What am I doing in that country?" referring to the region dealt with in the news. Of course I hadn't emigrated, but I was quite sure that in some way I had done just that. This, though not perhaps put into those words, appears to be quite a common feeling among people who have had major surgery, especially for cancer. I would suggest three possible explanations for this strange phenomenon.

First, the cancer patient, because of what he/she has lost, has a strong sense of being no longer 'whole', of therefore being different to those who visit them, and, indeed, from everyone else. There is, secondly, the belief at that stage that no one can share this experience - no one has ever been where I am, we no longer speak the same language. The third factor is more complex and appears to contradict what I have said earlier about partners sharing the trauma. There is a difference between being near death and being near bereavement. Eventually these two experiences can bring the nearly dead and the nearly bereaved closer together, but their experiences are fundamentally different and add to the cancer patient's sense of isolation, almost alienation, in the post-operative period.

However, in that context I have to say again how much I owe to Diane's love, support and courage. Only I know the toll it took, and I do so wish that people would talk less of what I went through and be a little more conscious of what she has endured - not just at the time when I was so ill, but in the years since. I was glad her mother could be with her during my time in hospital. Michael, too, was a tower of strength to her, although he had just been through a painful marriage break-up; Peter hates hospitals and illness and I cannot say how much it meant to me that he overcame all that and visited me often. My scars are visible; theirs are not. Many friends came to see me, although I cannot have been a pretty sight. My friend and former colleague John Waller, who by then was Bishop of Stafford, made a great contribution and probably does not realise how important it was. He saw to it that a bush telegraph was at work through which old, interrupted friendships were resumed through visits and letters. My room was so full of cards and novelty presents that, on the last day, Mr. Thomas said, "You can pack up your nursery and go home"!

A word about the nurses, and nurses generally. I remember them all well and feel a great sense of gratitude for their care, patience and tolerance of my cantankerous ways. A night sister made it clear that she had rumbled both my needs and my nature. One morning I woke to find a new notepad at my bedside in which she had inscribed, "For you to give your orders".

Patients in hospitals feel a special kind of dependence on nurses which makes us see even the youngest of them - and some are so terribly young - as mother figures. We look to nurses for comfort and assurance when we are in pain and frightened, and because we are in unfamiliar territory in which they are at home. It says much for them and for their training that most of them can respond to these unspoken needs. No one feels more irritated than I, when nurses call me 'Darling' or 'my sweet' or ask 'how are we today?'! But we bring it on ourselves. We cannot want nurses to be Mummy and yet expect them to treat us as professional adults. So they get into this awful habit of treating us all as if we were slightly demented infants. It saddens me to have to add that my experience of nurses 23 years later was significantly less positive.

I have kept the reams of scribbled notes with which I communicated with doctors, nurses, family and friends during the weeks in hospital. These notes are a souvenir of an 'interesting' time. They also remind me of the nature of my communication with people and of the medical procedures to which I was subjected - how I hated some of the daily routines; how I graduated from the ghastly plastic tube in the hole in my neck, keeping it open properly to the more elegant silver one with which I would have to live for many months; how I gradually learned to change the tube myself twice a day and how that hurt at first.

From the start I had been told that it would probably be thought wise, after my stay in hospital, to have a course of radiotherapy to 'encapsulate' and hopefully kill off any remaining cancer cells. In the event it was decided that I should receive daily therapy for five weeks. Perhaps because of the battering of the surgery and because I was feeling weary, I found this period a terrible strain and radiotherapy itself very unpleasant. After the first few days I believed I would escape the side effects about which they had warned me, but I was wrong. The nausea and slight burning did overtake me and in some ways I felt sorrier for myself than I had done in hospital. It has made me feel great sympathy for the thousands who have to undergo this, and the much more serious chemotherapy-type treatments, for considerably longer periods. On the other hand, if the G.P. had been on the ball in the first place, I might have escaped with radiotherapy alone and I would still have a voice box today. If! As they say, "If my grandmother had had wheels, she would have been a bus".

**Terminal**

The radiotherapy probably did do some good, but a few months later I had to report a lump in the side of my neck and found myself back in hospital, this time for a 'block dissection'. I was convinced that it would be quite a minor operation in comparison with the laryngectomy. That turned out to

126

be a slightly naive expectation. Cancer operations are not minor and this one left me without muscles in my left shoulder rendering me permanently unable to lift that arm properly and suffering from other rather tedious after-effects. I had, some would say, always been a bit unbalanced; now I literally had problems of equilibrium. It explains why I have since then found it almost impossible to execute a neat genuflection in church!

After this operation we learnt that Mr.Thomas had found rather a large number of cancer cells and that he was not totally optimistic. It was suggested that we might want to celebrate Christmas early that year.


At this point in my account I am no doubt expected to develop a theological thesis about death. I would only say that, however unnerving, it is not entirely a negative thing to have to face the inevitability of death in such a stark way. Most people do not have to do this until they are even older than I was at that time; and many are given no time at all to contemplate their death. Sadly, it often creeps up unannounced. We all know we are going to die, but somehow we are convinced that it won't happen to us until some time in the distant future and we can think about it then. I did not particularly enjoy facing its probable imminence. Yet in retrospect I am thankful to have been given a moment in life when there was a stark urgency to take stock of what I believed, what I needed to fear, and of what I need not be afraid. I had certainly up to that time sinfully neglected the discipline of preparing for death. And since you ask: yes, I believe in life after death; and no, I've no idea what that means.


It is of course possible to go into denial, simply to refuse to believe it is happening, or to accept the situation fatalistically. One can go to bed to die, wallow in self-pity and become morbid. The alternative is to fight, to say,

"I am not going to die; I've a lot to do yet and much to enjoy". Some will consider that this borders on the blasphemous, that one should quietly submit oneself to God's will. Of course, but God does not will suffering or sickness or bereavement and if He gives me the strength to fight these things then I am right to have fought. People say I survived through sheer bloody-mindedness. That is fine, as long as I myself do not lose sight of the source of that stubborn attachment to living.

So then, I may have a funny voice and a wonky shoulder and all sorts of other minor ailments, but I am alive and was very active for many years after all this and for that remarkable bonus I thank God and those who have put up with me and sustained me.

## Re-learning

Before my laryngectomy operation I had a visit from the speech therapist to explain how the operation would take away my voice and how she would afterwards be able to teach me to develop 'oesophageal speech'. At the time it was all pretty academic and deep down I believed neither her prognosis nor the hope she held out. As I have said, one cannot imagine oneself without a voice while one still has it. I am not alone in having sometimes tried to imagine what blindness must be like by shutting my eyes for a while; but of course blindness is so much more than that, and those of us with sight cannot imagine it. So it was with my perception of voicelessness. When Sylvia Paine, the therapist, re-visited after the operation, I began to understand what I had lost, but not yet how I could acquire something in its place.

At this time I also received visits from two former laryngectomy patients. I was so grateful that they took the trouble to encourage me in this way. It was, on the one hand, good to see how these men had learnt to communicate again, to progress from silence to the ability to make themselves heard. On the other hand, their visits provided my first encounter with this very different kind of speech and I found it ugly and frightening. I have tried to be sensitive to both aspects when I have myself since then visited laryngectomy patients before and after their operations. It is encouraging to learn that there is life after the operation, but a shock to find that one is going to sound like that.

The speech therapy sessions started within two weeks of my coming out of hospital and I shall always be grateful to the NHS for providing this service, for Sylvia's skill, and not least her tolerance of my impatience. I was determined to talk again, and quickly. Unfortunately, learning oesophageal speech is hard and slow and can only be done in short steps. It was a great help to both of us that Diane was allowed to be with me at these sessions. She was able to assist me more efficiently with my 'homework' and to support Sylvia's work of slowing me down.

So in those early days I had to learn 'TAH', and then two 'TAH's, and then three times, and finally, "please practice at home to five times". After TAH came TEH and TEE, TIE, TOE and TOO. Then very gradually we progressed to carefully selected consonants and later still to actual words, but not yet, not for a long time, any words beginning with a vowel. 'Stop' and 'flop' come after a while, but 'after', 'echo', 'uniform' are very much more difficult and always will be. The hardest are the inflections in voice, which laryngectomees are not supposed to be able to master but on which I arrogantly insisted. Thanks to Sylvia's enormous patience we were able to practice 'I said *No*', 'It's *under* the table' and, most difficult of all, '*Now*?' with the questioning lift of intonation.

Quite early on the NHS gave me a 'laryngaphone'. This is a vibrating instrument which is held to the side of the neck and produces sound when words are mouthed, but not spoken, by the patient. It is a useful way of communicating before some form of speech is mastered but sounds exactly like a Dalek from Dr.Who, I suspected that over-reliance on such aids is a sure way of never mastering oesophageal speech and I handed mine back as soon as I could. There are, sadly, some patients who resort to this aid for the rest of their lives, but they are glad of what it offers them.

I refer elsewhere to what I have been allowed to do with my oesophageal speech, and record my gratitude to those who have put up with it. There are, however, some disabilities that the laryngectomee tends to retain forever. First, he has great difficulty with aspirates and runs the risk of being thought to drop his aitches through ignorance rather than disability! This also means that he cannot easily laugh at jokes – the 'hah, hah' response is too much effort – and he should probably not try to tell jokes because to do so skilfully depends on a degree of inflection that he finds hard. He must develop a flat, dry style rather than the more hysterical approach. Nor, however well he masters minimal inflections of voice, will he ever be able to sing again, and for some of us that is a very real deprivation.

The laryngectomee cannot puff or blow or suck - there is after all no breath above the stoma in his neck. After all these years I still forget and try to use a straw or to blow out a candle. Then I wonder why those around me laugh.

Finally, of course, one has no sense of smell. I am thankful that I have retained the sense of taste, because I like my food, but taste is greatly enhanced by being able to smell what one is eating.

Such relatively minor disability does do wonders for one's power to emphasise - with the sportsman who has had a leg amputated, the housewife and mother suddenly blinded, the pianist with arthritis in his hands, the millions who have suffered so much greater a physical loss than I have. With them I share a prayer I found soon after my operation on a visit to Tewkesbury Abbey: 'Thank you, dear Jesus, for all you have given me, for all you have taken away from me, for all you have left me...' The prayer is by St. Thomas More and made me conscious of the paradox that losing something of great value can be a gift.

**Does he take sugar?**

This 'Does he take sugar?' syndrome is in some ways the hardest to take. Most men and women with any kind of disability will testify that strangers and chance acquaintances will treat them as if they suffer from every kind of disability as well as the one about which they know. If you are lame, you must also be daft; if you have strange speech, you are sure to be stone deaf; if you stammer they must assist you across the road. Above all, whatever your handicap, they must pretend that you are not there at all and talk about you to your 'minder'!

Of course, we treat foreigners in much the same way. If they have difficulty understanding our language, we assume it will be much easier for them if we shout at the top of our voice. In any case, they must be backward. Are they not, in Kipling's words, 'lesser breeds without the law'?

Much of this is understandable, however regrettable it may be. We fear the unknown and cover this up by assuming superiority. Sometimes we do it by being patronising; just occasionally it takes the form of aggression. The inherent decency and kindness of English people makes it a very rare thing indeed for it to be expressed by mockery.

Natural as such reactions may be, it is sometimes hard to bear. When I stop the car to ask directions from strangers, it is hurtful to see the fear in their eyes, their obvious desire to run away. When I engage some stranger in conversation in a way that would be acceptable from 'normal' folk, I resent being humoured. So I fear talking to strangers and am thought curmudgeonly. When I am in a shop with Diane and I ask for something, it is insulting that they turn to her to reply. Unfortunately, this is not confined to the ignorant. Quite recently, I was in hospital for a day for an investigation and in my presence a nurse asked Diane for my particulars.

I am aware that people with other handicaps suffer these things far more and that I have myself sometimes been terribly clumsy with the disabled. In any case, I have learnt that these situations are not my problem but that of the people who treat me as something from outer space. My real friends have always known that I am a bit strange, and oesophageal speech makes little difference to them.

This matter of public perception of the disabled must, however, not be taken lightly. We must not only come to terms with our personal difficulties in communicating with the handicapped. It is important to campaign that there are the right kinds of doors and means of access to shops, offices and homes for those with disabilities, the right facilities for the deaf and fair opportunities for employment. Great strides have been made in recent years through education and legislation but there is a long way to go. It is time everyone overcame the desire to ask the rather silly 'Does he take sugar?' and that instead, as a society, we assure that all its members, regardless of disability or handicap, are given the opportunity to live full and dignified lives.

# XI

## LIFE AFTER LARYNGECTOMY

In the four years following my operation many of our friends had to buy new address books because they ran out of space on their 'H' pages. In retrospect it is clear that we were, to a much greater extent than we realised or would have wanted to admit, in a state of denial. We were trying to run away from the inescapable and changed our address with terrifying frequency.

First we persuaded ourselves that I needed sea air and that Brighton would be a nice place to live. Then we found out that Brighton was an expensive place to live and Diane felt she was too far from all her family. So we moved to Worcester because one of her sisters lived there and it was near her other sisters and brother, who all lived in Birmingham. In the meantime we had lived in two Brighton addresses in less than a year. Michael and Janet then had our first grandchild, Stephanie, and we thought - and they encouraged us to think - that it would be good if we moved to Milton Keynes, where they were living. We had been in Worcester for a mere 10 months. Almost as soon as we had found a pretty awful house there, and the removals people had unloaded our furniture, Michael and Janet moved to Leicester. We returned to a different house in Worcester and lived in it for 22 years – our longest time in any one place.

The awful restlessness of those post-operation years was linked in my case to a sense that any useful life was over. I had used my voice to fulfil my vocation as both priest and teacher, and now I had no voice. I was quite sure that my usefulness to God and man was over and that my unattractive oesophageal speech, and my lopsided appearance after the block dissection, would repel everyone. I had been so positive before and after the operation but had then clearly lost hope.

At that point we discovered Old St. Martin's in the Cornmarket in Worcester city centre and were attracted by the beauty of the church and by the anglo-catholic liturgy- smoke and bells and all the trimmings- in which both of us have always felt aesthetically, sometimes more than theologically, at home.

We quickly 'clicked' with the Rector, John Everest, and we have continued to enjoy his friendship long after he left the parish. I owe my readmission to the land of the living very largely to him. Within weeks of our arrival at Old St. Martin's he explored the possibilities of my preaching again. Four and a half years after my operation I climbed into the pulpit, encumbered by an incredible amplification apparatus supplied by the laryngectomy society. On the second occasion I threw it into the church and continued to preach unaided. This was not some 'throw away your crutches' act of faith, but an all too typical expression of impatience on my part. At first it must have been a dreadful strain for the congregation, but through patience and love they attuned to my voice over the months. I have never ceased to wonder at their generosity towards me and their determination to join their Rector in my rehabilitation.

Soon after I had begun to preach in the parish – at the other church, All Saints, as well as Old St. Martin's – I was invited to take a share in the celebration of the weekday Eucharists and, after a relatively short time, to preside at the Solemn Mass on some Sundays. At first I had to concentrate so hard on how to use my 'voice' that I got some of the minutiae of liturgy badly wrong. In a church in which the presentation of worship is taken so seriously, this mattered and I was again overwhelmed by the tolerance of the congregation. John Everest is a perfectionist and I was often conscious of the vibes of irritation coming from him when I made mistakes, but he allowed me to persevere.

John's occasional impatience with those around him does not always enhance his popularity. However, for me it was refreshing to work with someone whose reactions to situations are sometimes similar to my own. If the church wants its priests to be professional in what they do, it must accept some intolerance with amateurish attitudes, whether in the work of fellow clergy or by the laity.

I like to think that over a time the balance shifted a little, from the parish helping to rehabilitate me, to my being of service to the parish. I am glad I was able to be of use in the interregnum and am glad that John's successor, Paul Collins, felt able to continue using me.

Over the years I found myself more and more involved in the services and there was rarely a Sunday when I was not taking some part in the Mass. It was a great joy that we were all also leading the worship in All Saints, the other church in the combined Worcester City benefice until it became a modern charismatic evangelical congregation under the leadership of an Associate Minister and more or less divorced from Old St. Martin's. When Paul Collins left Worcester I was asked to coordinate the services during the interregnum and I stayed on for a short period with his successor.

John Everest, as Rural Dean, had encouraged me to stand for election as the retired clergy representative on the deanery chapter and deanery synod, which gave me the opportunity to become more widely involved with the Worcester churches. I also, from the moment John mentioned me to him, received great kindness and encouragement from the then Bishop of Worcester, Philip Goodrich. I was glad that he felt able to use me with odd bits of correspondence that passed across his desk and other matters on which he welcomed my input.

His successor was Dr Peter Selby. His wife, Jan, made Old St. Martin's her church and quickly became involved in the life of the parish and as a server in the sanctuary. It followed that the bishop also came to the church with her when he did not have engagements elsewhere and they were both greatly missed when he retired in 2007. For me, he had become a friend, mentor and confidant and Diane and I have very greatly valued the friendship with him and Jan since their retirement.

Through John I became a governor of the church secondary school in Worcester. I did enjoy this renewal of practical contact with the world of education, but the experience did not diminish my reservations about the role of the church in secondary education. In some ways the skirmishes I fought there reminded me of earlier battles at Archbishop Temple's School.

We had joined the local Labour Party, as we have done wherever we have lived. Now party colleagues put my name forward to become a LEA-appointed governor at Elgar High School. Within a few months of my taking up that position I found myself elected vice-chairman and a year later became chairman. This seemed the right moment to resign from the governing body of the church school.

Elgar was exactly the kind of school to which I have always been attracted. It drew from the socially more deprived part of the city and had a disproportionate number of less able students. It struggled to convey to the community at large how very successful it was, both in 'adding value' to those who would not have achieved too much in terms of traditional indicators like examination results, and in the excellent attainments of the more able students. The school also had reason to be very proud of its exceptional tradition of pastoral care.

During my years of chairmanship, the governing body had to address some nightmare scenarios which it is not appropriate to describe here. I was very fortunate to have had as colleagues a very disparate group of men and women who shared a great enthusiasm for the school and were unstinting in the support they gave it.

My views on education are set out in my book *From the Head Upwards* which was published in 2001 and is, of course, totally out of date as a result of the vandalism wrought in the comprehensive school system, first by the Blairite philosophy of the 'New' Labour government and latterly by the Tory ideologies and their education secretary, Michael Gove whose fanaticism one can charitably only describe as bonkers. So, inevitably, Elgar has become an Academy school under a new name and most of what we stood for has been wilfully destroyed.

Once I had 'retired' from Old St. Martin's I was able to continue the odd educational consultancy work and I was invited to chair school admission appeal panels for the County Council, which I found interesting and rewarding and in which I was fortunate to make good friends with the County's officers involved and several of the excellent people who sat on the appeals panels with me. Again, as at church, I marvelled at the tolerance shown by them all to my speech problems, not least by the appellant parents who came before us.

The celebration of the 50th anniversary of my ordination in 1999 and the 60th ten years later were great highlights for us and the parish. We were so grateful that Peter Selby preached at both and also presided at the latter. In 1999 he noticed the shape of most of the gifts friends had brought for me and in his sermon explained that 'we work our retired clergy as long as possible and then we pickle them in alcohol'.

From coming to Worcester feeling very alone and of no great use, we enjoyed many positive years, making many friends and learning new professional skills, Diane has also found a very satisfying and fulfilling life - first with the WRVS at the hospital and now for many years as a volunteer at St. Richard's hospice. She has of course been happy to be near her sisters and brother and sees t hem all regularly. By 2008 we had been in Worcester 21 years and on the whole felt that life had been good to us.

# XII

## AND THEN SUDDENLY...

On the evening of 26th September 2008 I was going upstairs in our house in Kenwood Avenue, our home since 1987, when I collapsed a few steps from the top. Fortunately I didn't fall down the stairs but of course Diane couldn't shift me from that precarious position and called 999. They sent a paramedic who was able to put me to bed and then left! I was aware of complete inability to use any of my limbs and realised that I was very ill. However, after about an hour I was able with difficulty to stagger to the bathroom where I again collapsed, cutting my head on the wash basin. This time an ambulance answered Diane's call and the two men tidied me up and put me back to bed. Nobody had suggested how I could receive the medical attention I obviously needed and an out-of-hours doctor for whom Diane phoned arrived at 2 a.m. She was utterly useless in diagnosing the problem or suggesting what should be done. Meanwhile I seemed totally paralysed and had no control over my body and Diane had no option but to make another 999 call. This time the paramedic saw that I clearly needed to be in hospital, where we eventually arrived by ambulance at 9 a.m. – but of course it was a Saturday morning!

It is difficult to convey what a traumatic night it had been, especially for Diane – I myself had only been half conscious of what had been going on. We had, I am sorry to say, been unlucky to catch the NHS at its very worst but once in hospital one at least got the feeling of being looked after. I will not dwell on the succession of X-rays and scans, the indignities of a unisex admissions ward over the first weekend, the ultimate transfer to the Strokes ward, the three and a half weeks of only minimal nursing by totally

140

overworked and, I regret to say, largely under motivated nursing staff, no visit by any doctor after the first few days, and some really splendid physiotherapy. I should mention the visits by a succession of volunteer chaplaincy assistants, some of whom not quite knowing what to do with a priest in my condition, others with weird theologies who felt they had to save my soul as they felt I was in some way 'possessed'! I was grateful to the hospital chaplain herself and her ministrations. But the fact was that I could no longer walk unaided, had no balance, was unable to write and had more or less lost my oesophageal speech, cultivated so laboriously over the previous 25 years since my laryngectomy. Life really was bleak except for Diane's daily visits (twice daily at first) but she, too, had been hit hard by what had happened and she was very worried about how our life could work out once I was considered able to return home and I was worried because she was totally fatigued.

The section of the ward I was in felt her unfailing visits were truly remarkable. We were a group of eight patients of whom one, Donald, an amputee, had assumed a sort of leadership (I called him our senior prefect!). He sensed when one of us was a bit down and made it his business to come over in his wheelchair and cheer us up; he introduced newcomers to the rest, and at times he became a militant shop steward if he felt the nursing staff was not giving us the attention we required. I heard he later lost his other leg at another hospital but some sort of confidentiality rules prevented the 'authorities' from enabling me to keep in touch with him. I so wanted to express my appreciation and support him with an ongoing friendship.

I was moved to 'Stepping Stones' at Timberdine in Worcester in the second half of October and was fortunate to be allocated a really nice room. I found the place a bit claustrophobic and I do not know how I would have coped without Diane's continuing daily visit. In the last 59 years we have been through a lot together, but the period at Timberlines took a greater toll of Diane's strength and found me more totally dependent on her love than at any other time. I was away from home 75 days and Diane did not miss a single one and must in total have driven to the hospital, and then Timberdine, at least 100 times! I cannot speak highly enough of the way the place was run, the hard work and dedication of the carers and the attention and help of the physiotherapist and the occupational therapist to whom it fell to arrange the liaison with Diane about my returning home. She was able to arrange such things as an additional banister and some bathroom grab handles. It was unfortunate and caused me further unhappiness that they were insensitive to Diane's worries about our being able to cope at Kenwood Avenue. The house was on a steep hill, the drive itself was at a very steep gradient, there was no downstairs toilet and it could not have been less appropriate for someone with the disabilities I now had. Eventually I returned home on 10th December and it was to be another ten months, after much searching and considering of options, before we were able to move into a spacious two bedroom flat in a high rise block provided by Worcester Community Housing, with warden support available if required and situated most conveniently for shops, transport and all other facilities. I move about with the aid of a three-wheeled walker and terrorise the neighbourhood on my mobility scooter, and on occasion we use a light wheelchair kept in the car.

We have to look back on our life as before and after September 2008. Everything has changed. At home I need more support and this makes heavy demands on Diane as carer. We can no longer go for walks, we travel encumbered by my various walking aids, we can only stay at hotels which offer rooms with special facilities. My voice, though gradually improved, is not what it was and people find conversation with me difficult. But I'm still here and life goes on – worship at Old St Martin's and the continuing friendships there, Diane's fortnightly stint as a volunteer at St Richard's Hospice which she treasures, the support she gets from attending the meetings of the St Richard's carers group, visits to the family, now more scattered than before, and even our annual week's holiday in Brighton which we enjoy so much. I have found membership of a philosophy group in the University of the Third Age stimulating and was even encouraged to lead one of the sessions. I spend many enjoyable hours at the computer and maintain email contacts with old and new friends; Diane has a laptop and plays Solitaire!! We plod on.

# XIII

## ...A JEWISH CHRISTIAN

### The survivor

When they selected some at the entrance to Auschwitz for the gas chamber and others for the labour camp, they did not use assimilation as a criterion. For Nazis, the men, women and children in those queues were no less Jewish because they had formerly thought of themselves as German first, Jewish very much second. Many of my contemporaries and their parents, from the sort of circles in which we had mixed before Hitler came to power, were in those queues and did not survive.

My life, as set out in these pages, could hardly have been less Jewish. Yet, if I had not had the extreme good fortune of being brought to England when I was ten, it is highly likely that a few years later I would have stood in one of those queues and been killed either in the gas chamber or from torture and exploitation. The sentiment common to those whom Hitler designated as Jews but who survived, especially if they survived with little or no physical suffering, is guilt. I was German and an atheist. I am British and a Christian. Yet I am a survivor among those who were seen to be Jews.

I feel the great burden of that survival; the burden that I lived at a time of holocaust and escaped. I have allowed myself, after what was done to six million of those who shared my race, to speak of reconciliation and forgiveness, when I myself have little to forgive and no authority to speak for those who were the victims. All decent people abhor what happened

144

and strive to eliminate the evils that give rise to fascism and racism everywhere. Those who qualified as potential victims, but were not, will share the irrational, but very real, guilt of survival.

By the same token, whilst most people deplore anti-semitism of any kind, only those who might have been the casualties of its most extreme manifestation in our time will share a mixture of revulsion and fear which is peculiar to them.

Before Hitler, people who had been brought up like me did not feel any particular affinity with professing Jews. It is perverse that it has taken Nazism to make me now identify with a racial group whose beliefs I do not share, with whom I have little contact, and who tend to see the way I have spent my life as little better than treason.

In Israel, Jews who are not religious have common ground in beliefs about nationhood as well as shared social and political concerns. They are all compatriots. The place of the Christian, the agnostic or the humanist who happens to be of Jewish race is far more complex in the countries of the diaspora.

## The Christian

The Christian Jew has an additional problem. History is peppered with the anti-semitism of the church through the centuries. Jews are blamed for the Crucifixion and have therefore been persecuted by those who proclaim Christ. I do not need here to stress the theological and historical complexities that give rise to such accusations or the injustices to which they lead.

The fact remains that such attitudes transcend the generations and even today most Sunday School children will tell you that the Jews killed Jesus. I still frequently hear '...and their children's children' quoted as justification for this tradition. It makes the Christian Jew feel vulnerable. He is, however, potentially a particularly sensitive interpreter of the Old Testament's relevance to the new covenant.

Every time I preach a sermon about the universality of Christ and refer to the Epiphany or the early conversion of the Gentiles, I am aware that in this regard I am different from my congregation. The events about which I am preaching have empowered their Christianity and define their own discipleship and mission. By contrast, I am in direct descent from the earliest Judaeo-Christian church.

**The wandering Jew**

Sadly, it cannot be denied that there are racial characteristics. No amount of assimilation, no conversion to other faiths, can disguise them, though they are perhaps less pronounced when people spend little time with those of their own race.

Physically, you cannot disguise being African or Chinese. I cannot escape from the shape of my nose, which is not unlike the caricatures of Jews in Nazi publications! I know, too, that some of my gesticulations are unmistakably Jewish. Such things have never worried me particularly and I cannot see that they have made me either more or less effective as a teacher or as a minister of the Christian gospel.

There are other racial traits. Few Jews have been outstanding sportsmen or women and, in European society, even fewer are particularly keen or effective handymen. There is a verse: 'Lord Finchley tried to mend the electric light. It struck him dead, and serves him right. It is the business of the wealthy man, to give employment to the artisan'. That tends to be the attitude of many Jews, even when, like me, they cannot afford the artisan.

It is the 'wandering Jew' characteristic of Jewishness with which I most identify. This may be because Jews are often immigrants and the more one is part of an adopted environment the more one is reminded of being a stranger. More likely it is due to the inherent rootlessness of a race which has been repeatedly forced to be on the move, from the earliest days of Jewish history to the persecutions of our own time.

Either way, I am rootless and restless; nor have I ever sought roots or rest. Having a wife and family is my only root, but with them I have wanted to move from one place to the next and emotionally I tend to live out of a suitcase. I could cheerfully live in a hotel and be able to pack my things and move to another one at a moment's notice, always provided, of course, that it is a four star! I feel attached to this country and love certain cities all over the world, but that is the extent of my identification with places. I cannot identify with the majority of people, who have a sense of belonging to towns and even to houses, notwithstanding what I have said elsewhere in this book about being a Berliner and a Londoner.

147

I look upon this characteristic as morally neutral. It is neither wrong nor right, nor can I prove that its cause lies where I have placed it. When I see Jewish celebrations, like the Passover or a boy's *bar mitzvah* I do not belong yet in some strange way I identify with it. There is no getting away from the fact that I am a Christian Jew, and not just a once-Jewish Christian.

# EPILOGUE

In *Desert Island Discs* – a Sunday morning radio programme, which has been running for very many years, the castaways were often asked what regrets they have, as they look back over their lives. It always astonished me that so many of them claim, like Edith Piaff in her famous song, *Je ne regret rien,* to regret nothing. Are they all totally insensitive or compulsive liars?

What do I regret as I look back over the life of which I have tried to give an account in this book? I most regret my clumsiness in my dealings with some with whom I have had contact over the decades. It would have been better if I had sometimes been in less of a hurry to achieve aims or win an argument, less selfish in some relationships. I fear I cannot regret that in some matters I have been totally uncompromising.

I also regret that I often did not avail myself enough of opportunities with which I was presented, and I wish that I had read and studied more diligently, and more fully used gifts I have been given.

Of course I look back with sadness at much of the history of the century through so much of which I have lived. I was born four and a half years after the end of 1914-18 World War, with its dreadful trench war and death toll. Throughout my childhood, and afterwards, one saw the victims of shell shock and gassing, men who had lost their sight, the amputees and those who had been widowed as young women and not ceased to mourn. Then there was the Spanish Civil War with its casualties and fearful outcome of fascist dictatorship. Several of my slightly older friends joined the International Brigade there and a number suffered greatly.

Since then we have had a second terrible world war, this time 'total war' - involving the sacrifice and suffering of the civilian populations. We have had Korea, Vietnam, the Falklands and the Gulf and the outrageous war in Iraq and the still ongoing conflict in Afghanistan; there have been innumerable economic depressions and several generations suffering from insecurity and unemployment; we have had racism and petty nationalism – from the civil wars in Yugoslavia to the fanatic Europhobes in this country. The catalogue of things about which we can rightly be depressed is too long.

Newspapers run interviews with mini celebrities in the form of questionnaires. They ask virtually unanswerable questions, like 'Whom do you most despise?', 'Who is your greatest hero?', and even 'How often do you have sex?'! I recall a sex education course in which I invited young people to ask questions. One cheeky young man obviously assumed that, at around forty, I was well past it and asked 'When did you last do it, sir?' To his horror, and the amusement of the rest, I looked at my watch.

One should not despise, though it is sometimes difficult to have much esteem for those who have played prominent roles on the world stage. Margaret Thatcher certainly ranks for me as the person who did most harm in peace time to the well being of society by denying that society exists. She set out to change this great country from a caring and compassionate community into a nation of greedy entrepreneurs and bigots and the recovery from the mischief she wrought will be slow and may only be partial.

But there have been many in this century whom one can admire and who made great contributions to the well-being of the world. They were human beings, so they had faults, but their good was greater than their flaws. Ghandi and Nehru, Churchill, Gorbachev and Mandela stand out for me. Unfortunately some of the history of Stalin's Russia has distracted attention away from the fact that the Revolution freed that country from the evil of the Tsars and that the Soviet Union made an honest attempt to make an alternative to capitalism work. So we have been encouraged to forget that Cuba is better under Castro than it was before, that Allende was a good - and martyred - leader for the people of Chile and that even Mao Tse Tung was better than Chiang Kai Chek. Those who strove to return the world to some kind of normality in the 1940's and 50s are too easily forgotten. In our own country Clement Attlee and even Harold Wilson, and abroad John F Kennedy, are among those who left the world a better place through their actions. And my personal list of heroes will always contain Aneuran Bevan to whom the generations since 1948 have to thank for the National Health Service.

Like everyone, I have private heroes among family and friends, and there are writers, actors, artists and broadcasters who have enriched my life.

In the church I have been inspired by a number of people and befriended by others to whom I owe much. My list would probably be headed by Archbishop William Temple. The particular relevance of his leadership of the Church of England during his all too short time at Canterbury made an enormous impression on me at the moment when I had to make important personal choices. Michael Ramsey, Mervyn Stockwood and John Robinson, Charles Crowson and, by no means least, though at a more personal level, Douglas Rhymes, all influenced me and gave me much for which I never cease to be grateful.

I recall with pleasure and admiration those whom I have known who have shown courage or outstanding kindness, and many hundreds of young people whose enthusiasm and optimism cheered me. No teacher's life is ever without the pleasurable remembrance of those whom we have been privileged to see grow up.

Perhaps above all, I am glad to have lived in an age in which we have seen unprecedented advances in science and technology in so many fields, not least in medicine. In my early childhood my grandmother was still suspicious of the 'new fangled' telephone. Who would have thought that before the end of the same century the Bishop of an ancient diocese and an octogenarian retired priest could communicate with one another via email! How can one look at the world in the 21$^{st}$ century and not marvel at all that has been transformed by our having the World Wide Web.

Mine has been an unexpectedly long life. Both personally and in the world about me there have been some very black spots, yet I hope I have managed to convey all the many ways in which life has been very good.

2401203R00081

Printed in Great Britain
by Amazon.co.uk, Ltd.,
Marston Gate.